D1245961

Z-ISMS

Insights to Live By

Matt Zinman

ZU Publishing, Inc.

ZU Publishing, Inc.
2110 S. Eagle Road, #346
Newtown, PA 18940

www.ZUpublishing.com

ISBN 978-1-7346781-0-9
U.S. Copyright Registration: TXu 2-174-317

For permission requests, speaking inquiries, bulk-order purchase options and/or international rights requests, email media@z-isms.com.

Obligatory legal disclaimer template ahead.
Thanks for understanding and respecting its necessity.

Cover Design and Illustrations: Matt Zinman and Nancy Lee Schnabel

Interior Design: Nancy Lee Schnabel

First Printing, March 2020

Printed in the United States of America

For my mom and dad,
Judie and Larry Zinman,
and in honor of
my brother, Dave.

Contents

Introduction

Not everyone has a book in them, but just about everybody has something exceptional within themselves that they've come to know. It might be a phrase of pointed advice that their parent or grandparent instilled in them. It could be what they find meaningful enough to put under their email signature or post on social media. Greater inspiration may come from a profound life event or experience over time.

What life lessons would you share to benefit others? What do you wish your younger self would have known? What steps can you take toward living your best life?

These are the key questions I considered as the driving force for *Z-isms*.

The very next question almost asks itself. What is a "Z-ism?"

Z-ism [Zee-iz-*u*m] (Noun)

> *Pearls of wisdom, original wit or personal experience shared to positively impact as many people as possible; Insights to Live By.*

What matters above all else is that *Z-isms* can apply to anyone who possesses unique insights that they want to make known for the greater good.

Z-isms covers a lot of ground by offering as much practical guidance as possible. It also reflects topics I've thought about extensively and experienced over many years. After reading, you'll come away with:

- unique approaches to self-discovery with a certain mindset to defeat unnecessary worry, anxiety and stress; ways to find and stay in your zone; and, straightforward solutions to ease daily living;

- original concepts to improve your relationships and interactions by sizing people up, seeing things differently, saving yourself from common hassles, eliminating needless assumptions, and better managing your energy;

- techniques to heighten mindfulness, such as learning how to go with the flow, harness gratitude, achieve your *why*; and,

- actionable tools and practices to enrich your life by winning the battle within, becoming a life athlete and maintaining self-accountability.

We'll also have some fun exploring topics like Making Coincidences Matter and the phenomenon about catching 11:11. All along the way, it will be as if we are having a personal conversation with a friend.

Together we'll walk through how to customize your Life Enrichment Action Plan (LEAP), track progress with a Self-Care Report Card and take the right steps to achieve personal growth to live your best life.

You'll find one topic builds on the next and that you may want to use a bookmark and take notes at certain points, especially in the last four chapters to allow time to reflect on what you have read.

As part of my commitment to provide you with a complete personal development tune-up, there are a few chapters that cover the essentials, including about mental health.

You'll also discover that *Z-isms* delivers on originality and advances some topics such as: the key to avoiding the wrong romantic relationship; that there are only two kinds of people in the world, one of which must be avoided or at least approached with caution; and how to amplify the Law of Attraction.

That said, the book also includes the need to share some personal stories, some of which had remained very private until now. So please accept my sincere appreciation in advance for permitting me to share those experiences with you.

Lastly, one major goal for the book is to keep it going with an exclusive and thriving forum for readers to exchange their own Z-isms. This also allows me to continue to interact and elaborate about certain disclosures throughout the book. In this way, *Z-isms* has no final ending.

So, if you want to share the amazing, profound wisdom and *Insights to Live By* that only you possess, I encourage and welcome you to join the Reader Forum and do just that!

Together we can inspire, support and accelerate our continuous, collective and individual personal growth.

With that in mind, if you get as much out of *Z-isms* as desired, please consider recommending the book to benefit others so I may positively impact as many people as possible. That's my *why*.

In gratitude,

P.S. Before jumping ahead to Chapter 1 about outsmarting unnecessary worry and negativity, let's get to the bottom of "What's with Zman?" I believe you'll find that the answer foreshadows some essential parts of the book.

What's with Zman?

It's hard to miss on the front cover. *Z-isms* is illustrated using a dotted Z with a line through it, another dot at the bottom for a left foot and a circle atop for the head. It may be less evident at first, but "Zman" appears to be running in a cheerful, energetic manner. Can you see him? Some might say that he's "marching forth."

Anyone who knows me knows there's a certain meaning to the likes of Zman. He's no accident. In fact, his origin dates back to 2007 in a coffee shop in Newtown, Pennsylvania. More on that in a moment.

 The dotted Z originated as part of the brand logo from my first company, founded in 2002. Z Communication, Inc. was a marketing and communication firm with the tagline, *Connecting Expression with Impression.* For fellow geeks out there, that phrase represents the Shannon-Weaver Model of Communication, which is better known as the "sender-receiver feedback loop."

The dotted Z was meant to signify the science of communication and the strategic planning process of the firm. To complete the logo, the Z symbol used the backdrop of a paintbrush stroke to represent the art of our communication practices. We even named the logo, "The Swash."

 In 2005, when I launched "Z University" to venture into the world of internships and education content, I decided to continue with the dotted Z as a brand asset for the new company. In hindsight, using that brand made the wrong impression in an academic-driven market and was quickly abandoned in favor of founding a nonprofit: The Internship Institute. *Backstory complete.*

 Two years later, I'm in that coffee shop – working, wearing headphones and minding my own business – when a strange woman tapped me on the shoulder. I looked up to see someone in eccentric clothing.

Honestly, she was more like a costumed gypsy out of an old Hollywood movie. She'd either been looking over my shoulder or was passing by and noticed something that had the dotted Z on it.

Things got a little awkward. She didn't say a word. Instead, she smiled at me in a familiar way, reached down and actually took the pen right out of my hand. She proceeded to draw a straight line through the Z, add the dot at the bottom and the circle at the top. Right away I could see that it looked like a man in motion.

Right away I could see that it looked like a man in motion

I looked back at her. She had this look of satisfaction as if her work was done here. She handed me my pen back, smiled knowingly, and strolled off as mysteriously as she had arrived. Again, this happened without her saying a single word.

For as detailed and intense as that description may have seemed, it all happened in a matter of seconds. It was 100 percent bizarre and is 100 percent true. Yet, there he was. Zman was born!

Naturally, all these years since that unusual experience, there have been a number of opportunities for potential uses with my focus on the nonprofit. I have tried him out in various ways with programs and education campaigns. He just never seemed to belong. There's also an idea for a version of him as a tattoo. I haven't quite figured that one out yet. More recently, I gave him another chance in a handful of social media posts and memes, but it felt like a forced fit and still left Zman with nowhere to be.

Then came the opportunity and motivation to do the book along with the idea for the title. It finally seemed that he had a chance to come in from the cold. Zman's saga continued! Of course, that would be less likely without some "Z-themed" title. Seeing him on the cover just fits. I am stoked about him finally finding his home!

First and foremost, thank you for indulging me with that brief story. I admit to having a strong affinity for how those logos evolved because they symbolize my entrepreneurial experiences in conjunction with them, including with the book.

It has to come from somewhere and happen somehow!

Seeing how the front cover turned out, I can point to new symbolism, including the starburst around Zman, which represents the ripple effect *Z-isms* will have as he exponentially positively impacts more people. Did we just decide to make that up and assign meaning to it? It has to come from somewhere and happen somehow!

Now that Zman has come to fruition, my curiosity has returned to his point of origin and that encounter with my mysterious gypsy woman. What I find most striking is how that event and those since are analogous to the core themes in the book.

She drew him without hesitation as if he was there all along. Was that the moment he was born, or is that moment just happening now with publishing the book? Is it possible that that very instant she brought him to life became a foregone Inevitability that he'd see the light of day? Now that he's out and about, what does his future hold? Could our unusual visitor have known that answer all those years ago? Granted, it's a stretch. Is it?

In this way, the book is a perpetual work in progress just like us.

Closing out here, thank you very much for placing your confidence in me and making *Z-isms* yours. I hope that you get the most out of the experience to carry forward and that it inspires you to join our Reader Forum and share your own insights to positively impact others.

Let's make a difference together!

#BeTheDifference

CHAPTER ONE

Earned Confidence

Every one of us identifies with having been through however much in our lives. What doesn't kill us makes us stronger, right? And here we are: still standing!

Earned Confidence, among other things, enables us to apply the logic of experience to spare ourselves from self-inflicted stress, worry and anxiety.

In short, if you know you've survived your share of life challenges, what is the point of worrying or being anxious about what you know you're fully capable of enduring?

Life happens. We don't have a choice in the matter. We all encounter crises that require us to summon our courage and fortitude. There are trips to the emergency room. People we love get sick or pass on. We all know our list of the big ones and the many other trials and tribulations along the way – break-ups, break-downs and detours notwithstanding.

Take stock. Those life experiences also instill in us the ability to rely on our Earned Confidence. This also includes giving ourselves the benefit of any remaining self-doubts. We already know that we have made it to the other side of everything we have been through in our lives to date. So, it stands to reason that we can and will handle whatever comes our way because that is what we have always done.

Knowing and believing that, we have a logical question worth asking ourselves: Why worry, be anxious and stress ourselves out about things we don't yet know will happen?

That's a lot of unnecessary negativity and wasted energy! We know we will be just fine by staying in the present, taking things as they come and dealing with the real. Avoid the "what ifs" and stick with what is. We can deal with whatever comes our way and just live in the now.

> *Avoid the "what ifs" and stick with what is.*

Make the decision to trust yourself on this fact. If you're a "worrier" and still feel conflicted, push back. There's a habit to break. If you're content to believe, "well, that's just how I am," then it may benefit you to challenge that notion in relation to any self-destructive tendencies. Why be anything less than kind to yourself? You may also feel some baggage about past regrets or events you have yet to overcome. Those are different matters. Is this making sense yet?

Earned Confidence
(Noun) [Urn-d-kon-fi-d*u*hns]

> *An undeniable logic filter based on one's life experiences that proves it unnecessary to worry, be anxious or make assumptions about uncertainties because one is fully capable to cope with actual occurrences in real time.*

Why be anything less than kind to yourself?

This is not to say we shouldn't anticipate certain things and take precautions to prevent them. We'll cover that more in a bit. We can also brace ourselves for the difficulties we know lie ahead while doing so in a less painful, matter-of-fact way instead of prematurely draining others' and our emotional and physical energy.

Earned Confidence is a logic filter that enables you to decide that you have already proven yourself to yourself in the fact that you will deal with whatever comes your way when and if "it" ever happens. If this point is beginning to sound redundant, that's a good thing.

Of course, your sources for confidence are not exclusive to having survived so much hardship or being older. In fact, when people think of building confidence, it has more to do with major life events that filled you with pride. The tendency here is to point to experiences of proving yourself to others and the praise they gave you. Don't get me wrong. Being appreciated is great and it feels awesome. However, these examples tend to be more transactional.

When we consider the true foundation of this facet of Earned Confidence, let's revisit some major events in which you have proven yourself to yourself. How would you answer the question that asks what you think are your three defining moments or life events?

There are a few ground rules to this one. Your answers are limited to you, which is to say this excludes events like meeting the love of your life and your kids being born. In using the term "defining moments," it likely refers to things that happened in your formative years, including into young adulthood.

This doesn't have to be as a small child, but almost surely those prior to you considering yourself to be a fully formed adult. Again, we're leaning toward confidence-builders with positive outcomes and what has shaped you. Lastly, this is not just about the quick answer. Consider the reasoning behind those answers.

Are your defining moments coming off the top of your mind, or are you stumped?

Fair enough, here's my crack at it. Just before my 8th birthday, I was at my first summer clinic to learn how to play ice hockey. During one of the drills, an 18-year-old player took a slapshot and launched the puck with a left curve into that side of my face and broke my jaw in 3 places. My poor mom!

This defining moment doesn't seem to be off to the best start. However, the positive outcome is that, even with something that serious and painful, I didn't quit playing. It was important to me to not give up. I proved to myself that I am resilient. Continuing to play remains among my life's greatest joys.

The second example is also hockey-related. My teammates of the Temple University men's team elected me Captain my junior and senior seasons. In that last year, we went on to become undefeated champions. It was the final game and we were down by a few goals. We made a late comeback and the buzzer went off. It was that moment that defined the entire team. Right then, all of us rushed onto the ice, celebrating and jumping all over one another.

We were just a club team but it felt more like winning the Stanley Cup. It wasn't just the elation, it was the comradery. I didn't have many close friendships at that time and I never experienced that kind of bond. I harbored a lot of doubts about myself and that confidence boost helped me get past some of those insecurities.

The last example is my fourth internship in my senior year when I worked with a small public relations agency in Philadelphia. While my other internships were great experiences, this is the one where I proved to myself what I could do in my field of choice. Of course, I was still a novice. That Earned Confidence was validated when they offered me my first job. One of my mentors there also helped me secure my next two jobs which, combined, spanned the first 10 years of my career. That formative experience also instilled within me a deep appreciation for the value of internships, which is at the heart of my life's work that's still just getting started.

When you combine these types of positive experiences with all the hardships you've endured, it becomes even easier to truly know and say, "I've got this!"

It's incredibly freeing if you think about it and even more so when you decide not to worry or be anxious about something and assume that everything is okay. When concerns come to mind, call them out. Is it something that is actually happening here and now? Am I 100% certain my worry is valid, which is to say it is guaranteed to happen if it hasn't yet? Is it imminent and/or inevitable?

It's incredibly freeing if you think about it, and even more so when you decide not to worry and assume everything is okay.

Many people have a very active inner monologue. It may take a lot of energy to combat that negativity. For whatever reason, some people may avoid their inner thoughts. Does this mean your subconscious runs rampant? More importantly, what will you do about that answer?

It's important to acknowledge that this is in no way intended to minimize what has already happened to you or be expressed with any lack of compassion. Life is hard at times. It is also harder for some more than others. There is a reason why coping skills are *skills*. Even still, when challenging times come our way, it is completely logical to know that there is just no other way but through them and that the rest comes down to how we handle life's speed bumps, hurdles and barriers.

Applying your Earned Confidence can be effective in just about any life event regardless of its size or scope. It may be in anticipation of something good or bad that might come in today's mail. Just wait until the mail comes. Maybe it's a check instead of a bill. Anticipating events positively and maintaining that expectation is a good thing. Do yourself a favor and replace your worry with hope whenever possible!

> **Do yourself a favor and replace your worry with hope whenever possible!**

Something more than an everyday occurrence could be a medical situation, like needing to have a biopsy just to be sure everything is fine. Then you have to wait however many days to find out if lab results are benign or if you need one of several treatments with varying degrees of invasiveness, physical pain and recovery. That's a tough one, but you do have the option to make a conscious decision to expect the best and know that you can deal with the worst.

Start building and reinforcing your Earned Confidence to prevent or stop yourself from worrying about something unnecessarily, or that you repeatedly play in your head in advance. Expectations matter. It could be an argument you anticipate but never have. Instead, you end up having a nice time when you simply trust that you will be fine, regardless of it happening or not. Unfortunately, Earned Confidence doesn't go as far as overcoming innate fears about heights, airplanes, snakes or spiders, among others. Yet it can still help mitigate or prevent certain negative feelings.

This is one of the main reasons for this being the first chapter. It's too important to miss or gloss over and it anchors the rest of the book.

Once you fully process it, you'll realize that Earned Confidence is more like a formula in terms of its undeniable logic. Think about it as you would science or math. It's precise. It's a fact. There's no arguing the point. The greatest scientists and mathematicians in all of human history have found it irrefutable. Is that convincing enough?

For practical purposes, we'll stick with calling Earned Confidence a *logic filter*. Now let's put it to use. Suddenly, for whatever reason, you recognize that you're beginning to feel stressed and anxious. You realize that you're losing control and are letting those worries take over.

Your task here is to literally outsmart yourself!

Screw that! Stop it in its tracks and shred it with your filter. Your task here is to literally outsmart yourself. Seriously, if you have overcome everything in your past, then you've reached the point of knowing without any doubt that you will overcome everything thrown your way.

Are you still fighting that battle within? Face it, something unpredictable and unpreventable will happen no matter what. You have no choice in the matter nor one to dodge it. Why not wait until it actually happens before putting your energy into coping through it? Decide to defeat stress, anxiety and worry instead!

Another worthy aspect of Earned Confidence is to let go of regrets. This form of stress can drain our life force even more than unnecessary worry and anxiety about unknown potential events. Regrets are also more likely to be suppressed under the surface, so the only way to let go is to confront the past and keep it where it belongs.

What would it mean to lose your baggage?

This is a very personal topic and one we can tackle individually by relying on those we trust most and/or by seeing a professional. In addition, we address the situation by not-so-simply deciding to put the past behind us. In most cases, aside from your Earned Confidence, similar wisdom and positive memories, our pasts often do not do us many more favors. What would it mean to lose your baggage?

It's here where I would like to make the one and only reference to some song lyrics that you may find strike a certain chord:

"You can spend your time alone redigesting past regrets, or you can come to terms and realize that you're the only one who can forgive yourself. [It] makes much more sense to live in the Present Tense."

Can you name that tune? The song is called *Present Tense* and is by Pearl Jam.

Thank you for that brief indulgence.

Ridding our regrets are but one challenge. Our brains are programmed through habituation. We are also likely to experience times when we are talking to ourselves and saying or replaying certain things subconsciously and involuntarily. This may involve beating ourselves up, or we replay negative events over and over and over and over again, senselessly putting ourselves through emotional pain. Stop the self-assault!

The initial challenge is that we often do not even realize it at all or until it has already happened. We put ourselves down or make ourselves upset over something without cause.

The fundamental challenge we face is that we're all alone here. No one else knows what's in our heads or how it feels. We all have a lot going on all the time. Our brains are wired a certain way at birth and, unique to our genetics, have been constantly rewired ever since by our experiences. That continues.

The recordings that replay in our minds are learned behaviors. These are inner habits that also cannot change by themselves. Here's also where to recognize that there's only so much we can control, including what goes through our heads, mostly unexpectedly.

Now what? First, do you think you realize what thoughts your deep inner monologue just put in your head? If you think you know that answer then it's probably not worth the effort to think any harder. The fact is that we couldn't possibly know that or at least be fully confident that our self-assessment is correct.

This may be where reflection can help you get to the root causes. Did you grow up being a worrier? What were some of the common themes? Might it have been about a parent's well-being or maybe some fear of abandonment? Once you get to the source and shift your consciousness you can then begin to recondition your mind. What do you worry about most here and now?

Be mindful of thoughts you allow yourself to think. When you feel worry coming on, try to let it go. Ultimately, worry is an expectation for what you don't want to happen. The same goes for recognizing and negating assumptions. We'll think this through when we get to the topic of prevention.

In the meantime, I wholly encourage you to confront yourself about prior assumptions being proven false. You can make less of them while considering the detrimental ones that you impose on yourself and others as part of managing stress levels overall.

Confront yourself about prior assumptions being proven false.

As obvious as it seems, getting better and better at something takes practice. This is especially the case when it comes to thinking more optimistically and less pessimistically. Here again is an essential application to trust your Earned Confidence within yourself. It all takes proactive conscious effort and habituation.

What does it look like and mean to you to see things more optimistically? At the very least, lend yourself the perspective to view things differently, even if you don't believe it right away. It's a lot like forcing yourself to smile. It feels disingenuous at first but does give you a slight lift. Soon enough, it becomes and feels real. Here's where the advice to "fake it 'til you make it" comes into play.

Lend yourself the perspective to view things differently.

This seems like a good time to share one of my favorite anecdotes involving an encounter with a gentleman by the name of Patrick J. Jackson, Jr..

Mr. Jackson was an industry superstar who I had the honor of meeting at my very first professional conference. We were in the field of communication management, more often referred to as public relations.

I must pay respect to the fact that Pat delivered on his reputation. I'm not sure if he was the keynote speaker, but I easily recall that his presentation was well-attended. It was standing-room only with an uncomfortable temperature in the lecture hall. Yet everyone was happy to be there and fully engaged to hear Pat at his best. Afterward was the typical "meet and greet" session in which attendees lined up, introduced themselves to the speaker and posed some follow-up questions.

I do not remember what it was I had in mind to ask or say to Mr. Jackson or even my reasons why. What I do recall is standing in line with 3 or 4 people ahead of me while trying to collect my thoughts. My heart was racing. I distinctly remember it being more like thumping almost loud enough for others to hear it. That feeling of having ones' friendly neighborhood police vehicle escort you to the side of the road comes to mind.

I'm not sure I'd ever been so nervous and the feeling completely took me by surprise. Of course, that didn't help matters. It seemed more pronounced as I got closer to the front of the line and each person finished speaking with him. I was wrestling with self-doubts and the fears that he'd think less of me.

On the outside, I would like to think that I maintained a certain degree of poise and professionalism. However, I must have acted timidly in mentioning something to Mr. Jackson about the importance of the time he was about to take to speak with me.

In that very moment, Pat went to one of his favorite "go-to" impact lines. With a certain mentor-like tone, he asked, "Well, isn't this your time too?" I may have stuttered briefly but I acknowledged that I understood this to be both his and my time. He replied, "Well, if this is both our time, I don't see why my time is any more important than yours. Now, what's your question?"

> *I'll always remember how good that made me feel and how my nervousness suddenly just washed away.*

I'll always remember how good that made me feel and how my nervousness suddenly just washed away. That man changed my life right then and there. Even more impactful is that he gave me the gift of being able to do the same for others.

When I called GoDaddy to buy the Z-isms.com domain, the good-natured rep said, "I'm only 21." I knew at that moment that I had the opportunity to remind him he has a lot to bring to the table, no matter his age. I always enjoy paying that forward. I could tell he took it to heart and he thanked me.

At this point, I've probably relied on that humility check with dozens of others over the years and that's all thanks to Pat. It's the same thing I advise others in their career pursuits about requesting a conversation with someone they admire. If such an individual will not share 10 to 15 minutes over coffee, then they are the ones not worth the time.

Aside from my appreciation of that life experience with Pat, the point is that I held a perception that I was less important, whereas Pat appreciated me as someone eager to speak with him. He possessed the healthy ego to show equal respect along with humility and humbleness to emphasize his belief that we are no more important than any other person.

It may seem like a subtle example of how worry and assumptive thinking shaped my perception, but it was still significant enough to recognize that the actual circumstance was something much different. As a result, my nervous anxiety was self-inflicted.

Many of us do this often. It's essential to be mindful this is one of those instances that provides an opportunity to acknowledge that we got it wrong and that we will be best served by rightfully being more poised and confident in our approach to similar circumstances in the future.

This point is too important not to reinforce. Whenever you worry, feel anxious or make assumptions about a certain event that ends up turning out just fine, that's when you really need to step back and ask, "what did I do to myself or anyone else?"

Use that as a lesson learned to build and improve how you apply Earned Confidence.

That's a lot of inflicted negative energy. Acknowledge that it was unnecessary. Use that as a lesson learned to build and improve how you apply your Earned Confidence. Then, the next time you experience similar feelings, keep reminding yourself that you got it wrong before.

Thanks to earning confidence throughout my career experiences, I have no hesitation in approaching someone I highly respect. It may be because I would consider Pat to be more of a contemporary at this time rather than from the vantage point of being a new professional.

If you happen to be five, 10 or even 25+ years into your career, how much do you think your confidence has increased since entering the "real world?" What are some of the things that now seem routine that you would have found intimidating back then?

As a brief aside, if you happen to interact with young professionals, try to reconnect with what that was like for you and understand the opportunity you now have as a more seasoned individual to lift someone up. Be mindful to choose your words and tone more conscientiously to prevent unknowingly cutting them down. Do you remember your first boss or client writing you a note about doing a great job and how that made you feel?

More experienced professionals might think, "I'm just me." However, others who hold us in higher regard believe our words carry more weight. There's a responsibility to honor for that interaction. It's also important to keep in mind that there are a lot of "wise souls" in the world, including among those less experienced.

Rely on your Earned Confidence to feel secure that everything is okay.

Rely on your Earned Confidence to feel secure that everything or someone is okay. Know that any meeting, event or other concern on your calendar will happen as a "best case scenario." There is no need to overthink anything. Experience events in real time while trusting your gut and reacting moment-by-moment.

One other thought about Earned Confidence is to reflect every few years, or however long, how you've matured in applying it. Reassess yourself and decide. Then take pride!

It's understood that there's no substitute for experience and that our confidence is largely based on it. Even still, also consider what more you might be ready to do now that you may not have reached a level of ability in the past? What are your current goals or new ones that you are ready to set? What does it mean to step into your discomfort zone and achieve something? We'll want to revisit this ahead.

Let's not gloss over this point. Our self-image and our true identities don't always jive. The disconnect is mostly about self-reflection. I'm just going to wing it here. Just go along with me on this one if you'll be so kind.

Our self-image and our true identities don't always jive.

When I think of confidence, the very first person who comes to mind for me, as I imagine he does for many people, is the great, the irrepressible, Muhammad Ali. Most famously, those who know it think of his line, "I float like a butterfly, sting like a bee...," which he said as he danced around the ring while mirroring and taunting his opponent. But he wouldn't stop there, he'd keep going on all about himself and all his accomplishments, rattling them off as if they're weapons.

I think you'll find it worthwhile to put yourself in Ali's boxing shoes. If you were he, what would you say about yourself and what you've done to impress and intimidate your opponent? You'll want to pinpoint it succinctly and keep it to a single sentence. If that is too much of a challenge, then reconsider whether the accomplishment is important enough to you.

The other trick is that, no matter how much trial and tribulation factor into your life events and characterizations, what you say has to be turned into a positive something that either instills your opponent with fear and/or is shamelessly outright braggadocious about yourself. We're going for maximum positive thinking here and casting modesty aside.

First and foremost is to give yourself a break that whatever you come up with will sound nowhere near as good as the great one, and I don't mean Wayne Gretzky (gratuitous hockey reference accomplished). Alrighty then, I'm going to assume that you've either already attempted this exciting routine or you're somehow waiting for me to Walk the Talk first. Have you at least chosen your opponent?

I'll keep that one to myself, but will say, "I've battled and beaten two billionaires, gotten some of Bill Gates' money and was born the same day as the Broad Street Bullies." Like I said, it doesn't quite roll off the tongue. Disclosures and fun facts aside, all things being relative, it's going to be serious stuff for anyone. Some of it is totally positive and some may be mostly negative. If there's something to let go, then let go. The greater reality is that we're still going strong. Now what?

If there's something to let go, then let go.

Ideally, the main outcome of this exercise is that it will force you to reflect and confront how you would characterize your identity here and now, today. That begins to turn the kaleidoscope to update your self-image and close those gaps in your true self-identity.

We all grow. We get better at things. It's inevitable. The variable comes down to how conscious of a choice and effort we make to become something more and be however clear about what that earned destiny is to be.

To where does this lead you? How might this influence you to behave differently or see things through another lens? It's not as easy to be specific here. Whatever experiences you will yourself to do, make sure you recalibrate your plans to help yourself grow.

Give yourself a push. Maybe post videos on social media. Put yourself out there. If you think it's inevitable in that you will do it someday when you are ready, why wait? Making such progress is almost always harder at first. It gets easier and eventually becomes second nature. Can you tell I'm also psyching myself up?

In any case, I hope putting your newfound Earned Confidence into action provides an added advantage to overcome whatever challenges as they arise.

You got this!

CHAPTER TWO

Be Aware of Spiders

You've taken stock of your Earned Confidence. Now you can wield it to defeat self-inflicted worry and anxiety, among all else. Of course, personal development is not exclusive to turning inward.

It's also essential to focus on our interactions with colleagues, friends, family and in romantic relationships. We'll explore these in numerous ways from here on out.

One obvious challenge we all face in our exchanges with others is the simple fact that we are all so different. As hard as any of us work to improve ourselves and our interpersonal skills, the essence of who we are – our personality, temperament, values and character traits – are relatively constant. Each of us is a fixed point and everyone else is a moving target.

This means we not only have to be good at sizing people up, we also need to be adaptable. Here's where a social chameleon might come to mind.

We're not just talking about random daily interactions. This is at the heart of determining compatibility with whomever we choose to let into our lives and then how to navigate those different relationships every day.

We might try to hold back from judging people until we get to know them. Then again, there's something to be said about first impressions and trusting your gut.

It's hard enough to make sense of ourselves and yet we make snap decisions all the time to size up and classify the people we meet under various circumstances. Though we may not want to admit, each of us relies on certain judgment filters to some degree. In some - but not all - facets, it's human nature to evaluate others in terms of race, religion, gender, education level, social class, occupation, income, geographic origin, sexual orientation and political affiliation, to name a few. Take this the right way. I am not a fan of blanket statements, but the point remains relevant.

One instance that comes to mind is the experience of being on the dating scene and having a "checklist" to evaluate others for romantic relationships. That's an example with a unique set of criteria! Personally, as someone who's had my share of dating, I believe there's one checkbox that matters above all others, which I'll share in a bit.

Whether we gauge others by their demographic make-up or our personal checklists, many other aspects come into play. This brings us back to qualities that are less apparent, such as personality, temperament, values and character traits.

If only there were easy shortcuts to make sense of it all. They might save us a lot of trouble or validate what relationships to cultivate. Have you discovered any less-than-obvious ways to assess someone's core nature? Specifically, these are qualities that belong at the top of our checklists that fall into the category of "deal-breakers."

I'd like to offer some personal insights about a specific character trait that I've found is essential to distinguish among others, as well as within ourselves. Uncovering this is as much to our benefit as it is to prevent being to our detriment.

If you're sensing some hesitation, it's because what I'm about to disclose is characterized with some negativity. So just do me a favor and take a deep breath or two. I'm serious. Now, decide that you will not absorb the less-than-positive aspects of what you're about to read. Are you with me? Awesome! Here it is.

There are SPIDERS, and there are those who get caught in WEBS.

There are ONLY two kinds of people in the world – there are Spiders and there are those who get caught in webs.

Spiders are easy to spot in a work environment. They are those who play office politics and games that, in some way, involve imposing their will on others to achieve selfish goals.

They will manipulate others without any regard for the negative consequences their prey may suffer. They make a conscious effort to affect others' behavior to their strategic advantage. They pull your strings, yank your chain and perform like puppet masters. You get the point.

Fortunately, most of us are two-legged non-arachnoids. At least, I hope it is most. We know who we are just the same. We inherently trust others, unless our "Spider Senses" tell us otherwise. We live unconditionally and usually more positively. We would give others the benefit of the doubt if we were ever to have any in the first place. We tend to be kind and optimistic. We believe it is more important to believe in the good of others even while still knowing not everyone is always good.

We choose to view the world in brighter colors than our Spider counterparts.

Our integrity and self-respect motivate our willingness to martyr ourselves and suffer the consequences of those Spider bites. Our idealism makes us vulnerable, yet we choose to view the world in brighter colors than our Spider counterparts.

19

There are those who've been ensnared too many times to salvage their ideals. They are skittish. They reserve their trust until others earn it.

For some, being a good human being is inspired by religious faith. For others, it's about family, community and making a difference being most important. Regardless of our individual motives and willingness to unknowingly be web bait, we hope for the best.

Then again, you may self-identify as a Spider who typically manipulates others, and it may not entirely be your fault. This might lead us to consider the classic "nature vs. nurture" debate, but there is no 'versus' in the case of Spiders because it might be a combination of both factors. White supremacists come to mind simply because no one is born hateful.

> **No one is born hateful.**

Spiders are just that – Spiders! Even if only 1% of their behavior reflects it, the point is that they have it within themselves to intentionally manipulate others. It's an innate, singular character trait and a conscious decision people make to do or not do. It is a black and white truism, which is to say it's a straightforward characterization of other people and ourselves. Being aware is to our benefit and to shield us from harm.

I want to reiterate that categorizing people in this way isn't entirely all or nothing. Context matters in terms of our relationship to these individuals, the extent of our interactions and whether they'd ever turn their manipulative energies against us personally.

That said, it's important to keep top of mind that many Spiders also take satisfaction and even pleasure in "capturing" someone or multiple others with their deceitful, insecure, dishonest, contemptuous, conniving and cowardly acts. That's just to name a few. Contrary to those unsavory character traits are those with integrity who do the right thing while no one else is looking.

Sure, Spiders can *act* like the rest of us and blend in. After all, that is their nature.

The difference is that, once they decide to be cunning, they spring into action by weaving webs about how to manipulate whoever they can to get their way. They are saboteurs. Meanwhile, their prey is oblivious because their energy and mental focus remain well-intended.

Hey, Spiders! You *know* who you are! Yes, this question is for you: Do you take satisfaction at others' expense? It would be a mistake to be overconfident. Some of us can see you in plain sight. Let's capitalize Spiders just to call you out. The irony may be that *you're* the one who is unaware of your transparency.

Some Spiders may even feel legitimized when the culture of certain workplaces lend themselves to it, be that to get ahead or as part of a toxic environment. Some people consider themselves admirable for being cutthroat in business. They may view shrewdness as a source of pride in a competitive "dog eat dog" world, or just simply take pleasure in stepping on people to get to the top. These are those you might think of as a "wolf in sheep's clothing."

Do you know people like this? Do you think such behavior is acceptable? Your answers may be telling.

> ***Do you think such behavior is acceptable? Your answers may be telling.***

If you're in that work culture, how can a nice person not finish last? Should they be willing to take a slower route to achieve upward mobility and take pride in preserving their integrity? Maybe the better choice is to move on from a toxic environment in favor of one where good work stands on its own merits and stress levels are manageable.

For what it's worth, my consulting experience has provided a first-hand look into well over 100 companies of just about every type and size. Every single one of them exhibited a certain level of dysfunction, much like any family. The question then becomes one of belonging, adaptability, sensible expectations, poise, deftness and the all-important relationship with your boss. They're often in the best position to insulate you from others.

As with every non-Spider, I have repeatedly learned this lesson throughout my personal experiences. For me, sharing this has little to do with cleverness as it does practicality. I have thought about this for many years. Those consistent experiences have instilled me with the full Earned Confidence to "put this out there," knowing within myself that it is entirely true.

In short, this metaphorical view of the world and others as either being Spiders or non-Spiders makes sense and I believe you will find the same.

To be clear, the intention behind sharing this observation does not rise to the level of some epic battle between good and evil, though that correlation exists. This is specific to an individual having true integrity and strength of character in contrast to those who lack at least both and the underlying interactions among us.

Okay, now that the current World Order is, at least temporarily, defined by people having eight legs or two, the logical question is, "Now what?" Seeing that we have called attention to the topic, this new-found awareness works something like having a flashlight. The key is to know how to turn it on, use it, where to point it to see Spiders and anticipate the location of their webs so we steer clear of them.

First, be sure to trust your gut when your Spider Senses kick in. You may have concerns about someone but want to give them the benefit of the doubt and still believe in them. That's fine for now. However, instead of brushing aside those doubts, you can still be a good person with subtle suspicions and not think badly of yourself.

One way to recognize Spiders is by noticing that they always seem to have an "out." This is sometimes referred to as "plausible deniability." It is part of their typical scheme to know every hole into which they can crawl.

In a broader context, there are many reasons why people act like Spiders while others prefer to remain less aware and deal with events as they arise. Each possesses different values as incentives, though it takes a lot more energy to be devious than it does to be oblivious.

> **It takes a lot more energy to be devious than it does to be oblivious.**

What's more important is to go beyond reading and take this concept for a spin. Pun unresisted. In fact, consider pausing here for a thoughtful exercise. Think about the top 5 to 15 people currently in your life that you consider to be in your direct orbit. Now, do a quick run-down by posing a question and answering with the first thing that comes to your mind.

It's a straightforward "Yes" or "No" response. Are they a Spider or non-Spider? Who has it within them to selfishly impose their will on others and who is too good-natured to do such a thing? Put another way, is someone a manipulator or a non-manipulator?

If you decide not to pause here for that exercise, it's perfectly understandable and respectable to assert your free will. I don't want to be bossy but do encourage you to save it for later and see where it goes. If you did participate in this spontaneous Spider Senses exercise, what did those thoughts reveal about whomever you decided has the capability to behave in a Spider-like manner? This naturally includes family members, in-laws, supposed friends, coworkers and colleagues, among others.

Do you hold it against them or believe and accept that being a Spider is just in their nature? This correlates with the adages of zebras or tigers being incapable of changing their stripes. There's also an old proverb about the scorpion and the frog that suits this occasion, if you'd care to look it up.

To be fair, Spiders also come in different sizes based on the frequency and the lengths to which they will go. It should be pretty easy to spot a Black Widow wearing an Aunt Jane suit. If only we were able to choose our family and in-laws, right!

Still, the question remains: Now what? In any given life event where you find yourself taking a pause to evaluate something, no matter how ordinary or unlikely, that is when you stand to benefit from playing along with this exercise.

You can call it what you will. For one, it gives new meaning to *Arachnophobia*. If you weren't afraid of big, hairy spiders before, you might have a new opinion. Then again, you might find it humorous in some way.

Now that you have some added awareness and protection in being able to sense and combat Spiders, the key is to wield it properly. As much as you may master shining your light to reveal those approaching Spiders or nearby webs, you have to be aware that you cannot detect them all, run away fast enough nor anticipate their traps to remain uncaptured.

After all, who wants to go through life always being on guard and trying to figure out every which way to turn? It would consume a lot of negative energy. That's exhausting! Life would be much less enjoyable if defined by fear and paranoia. It's important to resist that temptation and keep your balance.

> **By design, being an idealist tends to keep one naïve.**

The point is that we non-Spiders prefer to be somewhat oblivious to others imposing their will upon us to their advantage and our potential detriment. We know that there are those around us who don't always have our best interests at heart, yet we choose to remain vulnerable. By design, being an idealist tends to keep one naïve.

Similarly, just to reiterate, a Spider may be among the nicest people you know. You may never be among their target prey. They might only spring into action on rare occasions or circumstances.

However, if they ever weave webs, they are who they are.

This brings up something that hits close to home, literally. We live in a new development that's run by a homeowner's association (HOA). In short, we govern ourselves. I decided to volunteer to serve on the Board to help my community get off to the right start.

As these things go, it has required a lot more time and complexity than expected, but we're well on top of getting the doing done.

On the flip side, there has been a mounting dilemma. People are people. The community has growing pains and the HOA seems to be everyone's favorite target. There's a steady stream of gossip, complaints, finger-pointing and bickering followed by more complaining. It's either about non-issues or making mountains out of molehills and mainly about things beyond anyone's control.

As the odds would have it, there are a handful of Spiders at work behind the scenes. To me, they're in plain sight. Yet they rile up others who fall prey to their webs and turn into their personal wind-up toys.

Over time, as more of nothing festers into something, the vibe in the community has soured, at least for now.

The Spiders have taken it upon themselves to poison the well and convince others to drink from it. They know who they are, as do I. I'm aware of keeping my shields up and shrugging it off. But my other neighbors – the ones I care more about – are unknowing victims. It's not the vibe they deserve.

People need to lift a finger before pointing one.

I knew volunteering to be on the HOA board would be a thankless position. People can choose to be ungrateful but I do not accept people being hateful. The irony is that if they only put half of their negative energy into helping out instead, there'd be no problem. We've repeatedly asked for more volunteers and no one steps up.

People need to lift a finger before pointing one.

The other irony is that there's no significant reason to complain at all. The neighborhood is in good hands. They could just enjoy their home-life instead of getting caught up in nonsense.

What would you do? Would you simply accept that "haters are gonna hate" and that it's pointless to reason with the unreasonable? Or, would you take a different approach?

Again, my main concern has less to do with Spiders as much as it does to free their prey. Yes, I'm disappointed in them, but I am more disappointed *for* them. This situation has been festering for too long. I decided to take it head-on at our annual membership meeting with everyone in the same room. It was the best opportunity to right the ship.

There's no way to sugarcoat it. Things went a bit sideways. However, I was able to raise the issue and make the point that we all didn't work as hard as we have to buy a home in a toxic community. We have a choice to either let this problem go untreated or to hit the reset button and leave the negativity behind.

I was proud of myself for exposing the problem – and, in subtle ways, the Spiders.

That doesn't mean they'll stop being who they are, but now that they've had a light shone on them, they may think twice before being less than their better selves.

> *People don't have to like one another to be respectful, kind and cordial.*

People don't have to like one another to be respectful, kind and cordial. We all share a desire to have a positive neighborhood for ourselves and our families.

This situation is occurring in real-time, which is sure to be the case about other life experiences while writing the book. The dust is still settling. I am beginning to sense that we've turned the corner. We'll see.

Now let's revisit similar situations you might face. Let's say you're in the thick of it, ensnared in Aunt Jane's web as she catches you off-guard. She prides herself on making you bend to her will. Or, maybe your boss is giving you a hard time for no good reason. They're the ones who are out of line for creating a problem out of thin air, but they're still your boss or a person with some level of authority. You feel helpless being in these traps.

Here's where to keep your shields up to prevent that person's negativity from getting through and inflicting emotional distress and mental harm. Your responses essentially need to follow the "sticks and stones" mentality. No matter who you are or where you're from, it's a pretty sure bet that you know that expression.

This is an Earned Confidence moment. Plant your feet. Hold your ground. Wait them out. Don't interrupt. Stay poised. Take pride in not letting them get a rise out of you.

This also may well be an instance when you're thinking or half-daydreaming of how awesome it would be to have this person occupy a smaller part of your life. Don't hesitate to use your Spider repellent when you are consistently, involuntarily, and environmentally exposed to some Spidery energy-sucker.

With that said, remember to stand up for yourself in that very moment! You are entitled to have your own opinion of any given situation or person, provided it does not jeopardize your current job security. They are equally entitled to think the same of you.

On the flip side of this circumstance, maybe you're the one being the only jerk in a particular case, hopefully unintentionally, or you're not acting inappropriately but they are just misperceiving and misunderstanding you. We all have that in us, even if it is something misinterpreted by the other person in a conflict. When confronted by such situations, it can be illuminating to shine the light back on yourself.

I have a reliable warning system for spotting Spiders. If you find yourself waking up at 4 a.m. with a certain stressful individual being the first thing on your mind, it's time to evaluate how to free yourself of them. If you are not someone who subscribes to the commitment to keep negative people at bay, then this may be a good time to reconsider your ideals.

This was the case with one of my former employees and involved spilling over into my personal life. Most of her performance issues and behaviors were subtle, but it was one thing after the other. I tried to give her the benefit of the doubt and see the best of each situation, but something was wrong. The negative energy was building along with restless nights. It reached the point of being involuntary. I was unable to free my mind of her and the situation. Can you relate?

It was good to be aware enough to notice certain things, but that also begs the question of what's not being seen in the shadows. Some months later, an audit revealed that she had embezzled some funds from the organization. It wasn't much, but it was enough to press charges. She eventually admitted guilt. Yes, there was some satisfaction in catching a Spider in their own web. It was also very sad to see someone so capable make such poor choices. For whatever reason, she lives life as a drama magnet.

We often do not realize how stressed we are until we experience relief.

Thankfully, this situation is now history. It was an ordeal. I am especially grateful not to have her occupying that real estate in my head. We often do not realize how stressed we are until we experience relief.

Stress is the absolute worst thing for us. We have only one go 'round and you have to ask yourself if someone is worth wasting your valuable time, draining your positive energy, and/or compromising your emotional health. Do you have a choice? Can you at least take measures to insulate yourself or avoid future traps? If ensnared in someone's web, what is the most sensible way to get unstuck and find the path to safety?

Another way to spot a Spidery manipulator is to recognize that feeling of wrestling with yourself about doing something for someone when you know you should say no to them. In fact, you're literally telling yourself, "I have to learn to say no." Meanwhile, you're beating yourself up for not saying no and resenting being manipulated by this person. Does this sound familiar? Can you feel the negativity building in the pit of your stomach yet?

This roots back to self-esteem. The reason you've become that Spider's prey is because they sense weakness. They know they can take advantage because you are prone to let them. In the extreme of dealing with a Spider-like bully, you've likely heard that the best repellent is to bully that person back until they back down, even if that's not in your nature. Many bullies act that way to overcompensate for their own insecurities, among whatever else. It's time to trust your gut and have the guts to say "no." In fact, this is a good rule to follow in almost any circumstance:

Value yourself first and the rest comes naturally.

Value yourself first and the rest comes naturally.

This was inspired by a situation with an intern who has been doing some projects for my nonprofit. I've worked with more than 300 students in my career and she's exceptional. I asked her about staying on and she described some of her other commitments she'd need to work around.

These included another micro-internship with some woman who has been having her do grunt work. She literally went to this person's house and was asked to move boxes, print mailing labels and the like while the woman took a shower. Meanwhile, her husband arrives home, engages this innocent intern about her work tasks and proceeds to criticize and upset her for something completely out of line.

Aside from the obvious inappropriateness of being in this person's house, the manual labor and being put in an uncomfortable position, she was unpaid and doing nothing meaningful. It was also taking an emotional toll on her. Meanwhile, she continues to feel obligated to this woman to do more of the same. She's having trouble saying no and is holding out for a letter of recommendation. It really burns me up to hear how this Spidery woman was preying on a good-natured college intern who I've come to admire.

> **She came away from this experience having learned to say no and take pride in her self-respect.**

I expressed to my intern that she's too good for this woman and is better off doing just about anything else. I then drafted the letter for her to send this woman to help her save face and escape. I was also happy to write her the letter of recommendation she deserves. Even if we don't have the opportunity to continue working together, I'm glad she came away from this experience having learned to say no and taking pride in her self-respect.

I think you'll find that being more aware of Spiders makes it easier to spot those in your life and the others you encounter so that you minimize how much they take advantage of you. This may hit close to home or at least to close family. Again, just because someone has it within them to act like an eight-legged creature does not mean they are spinning webs 100% of the time and that you always need to be on guard.

Spidery individuals tend to be selective about who and in what situation they'll come out of their hole. In my experience, most Spiders only show themselves 5 to 10% of the time, if at all. As good as you get at spotting them, they remain very cunning and can still be hard to catch.

On the other hand, if you happen to identify as being a Spider, there is still hope among us prey that you are willing and able to be less of one and instead choose to be your better self when dealing with others.

On an optimistic note is one other lesson learned from the HOA situation. While the experience exposed some Spiders along with other neighbors ensnared in their webs, there's another group who managed to stay above it all, or at least not fall prey. We've also become very friendly with several and are enjoying having those relationships deepen.

This also supports the notion of there being a subset with a third kind of person in this particular World Order: Non-Spiders who, with experience, can elude webs. Being like-minded in this way helps explain why we're all becoming fast friends.

More to the point, I've been trying to think through what sets this group apart. Let's have some fun here and call them dignified and deft "Web Dodgers."

If my young neighborhood is our petri dish to pinpoint this demographic, then I'd say that about 1/7th (under 15%) of the population have this ability. On a positive note, there's hope for others yet.

There's no one kind of anyone who demonstrates this behavior. For example, we know that it's not always age because people with "old souls" and the like have the poise to navigate through this sticky ground. I personally know quite a few people who are young in life with this ability in spades. As a matter of fact, one of my current interns fits this profile.

These Web Dodgers recognize that other people can be good at hiding their true intentions. But instead of expending energy being on guard all the time, they ground themselves with Earned Confidence.

They also have a clear sense about the many other genuine non-Spiders there are in the world. Our distinguishing characteristic is that we not only don't let such matters consume us, we almost don't give it a second thought. Part of this may be that they may or may not be adept at knowing for what signs to keep an eye out. Their strength is that they remain poised and deal with the situation in real time when any Spider reveals themselves by springing their trap.

Do you have any certain ways to spot Spiders in your life? You might find that some can turn the tables and put others on the defensive. They may be the one accusing you of something and making you out to be the bad guy, which brings guilt into the equation.

There's a fine line here because the dynamic of some families can be riddled with guilt. So if you find yourself on the defensive, then discern their intentions. A relative who gives you a hard time for being out of touch isn't necessarily acting with conscious intent to manipulate you. Then again, you can decide that for yourself.

Personally, the easiest way I've found to spot Spiders is by knowing whether they've manipulated others. It's that data point. If they have that history of taking advantage, then they have the Spider gene. I wonder whether it really is one.

In any case, even if you think certain people would never turn against you, they'll almost certainly do it again to others. That puts it in the realm of possibility that they could turn at some point. But you'll handle it. That said, be safe out there, stay clear of webs, keep your flashlight handy, your finger on the repellent and teach those Spiders a thing or two about not toying with you.

> **The good news is that it's onward and upward from here!**

As someone who takes pride in being positive and optimistic, it's been uncomfortable being negative and pessimistic about this topic. It took some hard living for Spiders to become transparent and it's too important to ignore.

The good news is that it's onward and upward from here!

Just spend a minute to reset, shake off any negativity and let's take a turn for the positive!

CHAPTER THREE

A Dose of Prevention

You are now armed and ready to spot Spiders and prevent yourself from getting caught in their deceptive webs. Hopefully, you are also emboldened by a fresh supply of Earned Confidence to prevent yourself from pointless worry, anxiety and stress.

Now let's consume a healthy dose of prevention to set the stage for what's to come.

Life is full of obstacles. Many happen unexpectedly and often knock us off-track and/or off-balance. We feel blind-sided. Sometimes it seems like it's just one thing after another and we're totally unable to catch a break. How can we stay on our game and advance the ball, so to speak, when we are being tackled from all sides? If it wasn't for one crisis or another, we'd almost surely reach the goal line.

Any number of things can arise and plenty of them are totally unavoidable. All we can do is deal with them. That's life. The ultimate question addresses how to get through each crisis and, especially, not make things worse.

Other times the reason why small problems become big ones is self-infliction. Then there are the rest of the times. Here's a good approach to maintain:

The best way to manage a crisis … is to prevent it from happening.

This has less to do with straightforward problem-solving, which applies to the present tense. To be clear, what we're addressing here is *pre*-problem-solving by working backward from preventing potential problems.

> **The best way to manage a crisis is to prevent it from happening.**

It also may seem natural to consider this topic in the same manner as what's commonly called contingency planning, but that's more about what someone would do to fully prepare for an event in case that event occurs. Think "fire drill."

What we're pinpointing here is total prevention.

Can you think of everyday items and actions that involve preemptive measures? Let's go with seat belts, phone cases, moisturizer, hand sanitizer, teeth-brushing, sports equipment, dryer sheets, hard hats, smoke detectors, vitamins, handwashing, sunscreen, insect repellent, exercise and other preventative healthcare, such as medical screenings. While mammograms and colonoscopies cannot prevent cancer, they can prevent that diagnosis from being made too late.

If you came up with boots, umbrellas and fire extinguishers, understand that those are contingency items that are meant to deal with an event that occurs. If only we could prevent bad weather!

What about habits and actions that are more unique to you? Here's one of mine that's a bit on the fringe. Get ready for some major personal transparency. I put petroleum jelly on my eyebrows when I play hockey. Why? It's because it helps the sweat go around my eyes instead of in them while skating. Do my teammates make fun of me? Not now that they've gotten it out of their system. Actually, I do still take some heat for it. After all, we *are* talking about bringing that into a men's locker room! Suffice to say, true friends keep you humble. Even still, I'd rather be weird and not care what my teammates think in favor of not having burning eyes that interrupt my gameplay.

YOUR FUTURE

Now how about we get in front of undesired, preventable occurrences. This is where we can pause and really confront ourselves and life's circumstances. First comes foresight. Can you identify something undesired that is going to occur if you do not stop it? What is your shortest line from A to B to prevent B from happening?

This is different from how Earned Confidence prevents us from being drained by worrying about something that's uncertain to occur. This dose of prevention is about positive practices to look out for yourself and others.

It takes present awareness combined with foresight and anticipation. As with many other topics here in *Z-isms*, it takes practice. It then takes present actions to alter, avoid and ultimately prevent undesired occurrences. Could something have to do with your "Spider Senses" kicking-in? Inventory the main happenings in your life and do some risk assessments. What is within your ability and free will to mindfully do or not do something that could possibly spare you and others the grief of allowing it to happen? Keep in mind and be kind to yourself knowing that almost nothing is a mistake unless it happens twice.

> *Almost nothing is a mistake unless it happens twice.*

Now that we've isolated what can only be described as flat-out mistakes, applied prevention cannot be overstated for taking whatever measures that can head off major problems.

Here's where this topic is especially important for anyone in relationships and applying a dose of prevention when it comes to assumptive thinking. By "cannot be overstated," I mean that it's too important to save ourselves from being in jeopardy of assumptive behavior becoming a relationship-killer. This can involve having "phantom arguments" about false assumptions by one or both individuals.

This also goes well beyond relying on the logic of Earned Confidence to just deal with the real. Whenever any assumption comes into question, as with unsubstantiated events, we must consider an essential question:

Is this something that is happening now or unquestionably certain to happen versus being an assumption in disguise?

These issues relate to learned behaviors. It's easy to point all this out about Earned Confidence, unnecessary worry, minimizing anxiety and stopping oneself from making assumptions to avoid the angst in its wake. However, these phantom problems elevate in importance when it comes to preventing the derailment of a good thing with someone special before something goes very wrong. I've had this happen.

Everyone seems to have a hot button when it comes to being accused of something they didn't do and being told by a loved one, "I don't believe you," when they're telling the truth. That's an indication that a lack of trust is degrading into contempt, which often is unrecoverable.

> *If you identify with these symptoms, you'll benefit by taking them head on.*

These behaviors can also spill over into other relationships. People have residual emotional energy from their own experiences and pre-perceptions that factor into interactions with others. If you identify with these symptoms, you'll benefit by taking them head on.

Now to the *how* of it all. There's the time-tested approach of using some form of behavior modification to break the assumption habit. It doesn't need to be the typical example of snapping a rubber band on your wrist. Then again, if that appeals to you, feel free to make each snap sting based on your own judgment of how unnecessary your assumption is or the severity of any other behavior you are aiming to improve.

Another practice is a reflection exercise, which comes into play once any self-contained life event or routine occurrence actually happens. In other words, you failed to prevent it. The ongoing question should be whether you can catch yourself in an assumption. Though it's way too often after the fact, all of us are familiar with doing this.

Hit the rewind button in much the same way we discussed building Earned Confidence. It's important to confront whether you unnecessarily put yourself or others through some level of negative experience and interaction only for things to turn out differently than what you eventually realize were false assumptions and/or preventable events.

Think about it. How much energy did you expend based on any negative assumption? What could you have done to have prevented that event from happening?

How much energy did you expend based on any negative assumption?

Confront yourself about prior assumptions being proven false so you can make fewer and less detrimental ones that you negatively impose on yourself and others. This point is somewhat a generality. A lot depends on the relationship, communication styles and the seriousness of any given assumption.

There's also mitigation. Whenever you fail to avert something that's actually preventable, turn your attention to your fallback position to prevent further damage. Let's say that a fight breaks out. Now the focus is to avoid rehashing the event with the person or people involved and doing whatever is necessary not to involve others.

Be respectful not to bend a lot of other ears unless it's absolutely necessary. All that does is perpetuate negativity and stress.

Have you come up with any other examples of events you want to avoid and how to stay out of trouble? How about hiding a magnetic key under your car or doormat; putting salt on a pre-storm sidewalk; baby-proofing your home; knowing and securing all your passwords; protecting your identity from being stolen; changing your car's oil before the engine seizes; placing solar shields on your windshield on a hot day; taking out an insurance policy on anything; or the all-important doing back-ups of your phone and computer.

For what it's worth, one exception to consider about these routine preventive measures is whether to buy warranties on consumer goods. It seems like everything comes with a premium offer to extend a warranty or insure an item. These can be expensive and are often part of some pushy salesperson trying to pad profits. Personally, I've found it makes sense to cover high-value items like phones and computers. Aside from those, I take a pass on every other offer. The strategy is that, while something may break at some point, it will cost less to replace than how much I saved by not getting all the other warranties. I guess that's my savvy shopper tip for the book.

Other than that, do yourself a favor and stop saying, "I'll get to it" before you're too late.

> *Do yourself a favor and stop saying "I'll get to it" before you're too late.*

One final word of caution that's literally for the road: make the decision to not allow yourself to text while the car is in motion. If you can't help but check your phone, wait for a stoplight. Lecture over.

Another related example happened when I was four years old. I found a can of bug spray lying on the floor of the garage and wanted to do a good deed for my mom by using it to clean her car tires. I was 4 at the time! My skin absorbed some of the residue and I breathed in too many of the fumes. My mom, unaware of why I fell ill, took me to our family doctor who diagnosed my symptoms as typical. She knew differently. Something was very wrong with her child and she rushed me to the Emergency Room.

I will never forget bouncing on her shoulder as the hospital ceiling lights flew by and my getting sick all over her. My fever shot up to 106 degrees and they put me in ice to get it under control. My mom trusted her instincts and saved my life that day. I would have preferred that spray can to have been kept in a safe place and out of reach. If you have small children, it might help to re-review your baby-proofing checklist.

Take inventory. What undesired events have occurred for which you can take precautions here and now to prevent? What's on your calendar and do you have your bases covered? What other vulnerabilities come to mind? Take the trouble to do these things now and you may well save yourself plenty of hassle later.

This is the one where we refer to life being too short and able to turn on a dime.

Let's go one extra step here by pulling back from everyday doses of prevention and looking at the bigger picture. This is the one where we refer to life being too short and able to turn on a dime, as the sayings go. This is somewhat abstract because it is so unique to each of us and involves big ticket items in the sphere of life. The one example that comes to mind is my decision to ride a motorcycle as well as to wear a helmet.

The first decision was based on a conversation with my mom some years back who was not a fan of my riding. That's what moms are for. I made her a promise that I kept, which is that I would wait until I was at least 35 before getting a bike. The reason was based on the logic that younger men often take greater risks and I was no different. Agreeing not to ride a motorcycle was a sound decision. I wanted to be sure I was mature enough to ride with my head on straight and not be reckless. For what it's worth, I'm partial to back country roads and only ride when mentally sharp. And, yes, as a parent now myself, I choose to wear a helmet.

Prevention runs the gamut. It's one of the broadest topics to cover and yet pinpoint distinct applications, all of which ultimately come down to our awareness and presence of mind. Here is where prevention intersects with mindfulness, which enables us to continuously solve problems by knowingly preventing them.

As a brief aside, I'd like to reiterate the point that the simplest and best dose of prevention when interacting with others may be simple acts of kindness. What comes to mind here is to 'Do unto others as you would have them do unto you.' Or consider that "You catch more flies with honey than vinegar." We're now in Karma territory.

Again, timing matters a lot. One thought that comes to mind is with my wife, Erica, and her daughter, Greta. When Greta first comes home from school, the odds are pretty good that she's on the tired and cranky side. Then there's Erica who may be overeager to remind Greta to clean her room. That's when I might remind my wife not to "poke the bear" and that it's in everyone's best interest to wait until after dinner for her to ask Greta about when she plans to straighten up her room. This may seem like a minor example. Trust me, it's far from it. Fellow parents, are you with me? Greta also appreciates that I sometimes run interference to avert an argument.

These same principles apply when it comes to interpersonal dynamics. Prevention begins with being true to yourself. For instance, it involves being honest about knowing what you do *not* know, knowing what you *know* you know and knowing what you *think* you know.

> **Prevention begins with being true to yourself.**

This is about more than factual knowledge and personal experience. It also draws upon self-reflection and your ability to help others interact with you. Can you think of something about yourself that routinely you tell people to help them better understand you?

For example, I sometimes admit to having "man brain," which is to say that I am incapable of doing two things at once. I'm hard-wired! It's so pronounced that, when I'm in a conversation with someone, I am not able to hear how I come across to them. I literally have to replay my words back to myself after the fact as if I said them to someone else in order to accurately "hear" the impression I'm making.

It's important to me for others to know this because I don't want anyone to take offense if they perceive me misspeaking or interpret my tone of voice in some way other than intended. A little self-deprecation goes a long way to instilling trust in others. Here's where poking fun at myself to disclose a personal fact is a dose of prevention. Then there are the times when I say the wrong thing having nothing to do with that limitation. We all make mistakes.

Now go back to what you might say about yourself and how to turn that to your advantage when you explain it to others. It's essential to rely on humility to hedge that variability, especially when it comes to yielding to the greater expertise of others. In the workplace, you will earn more respect and influence because people will find you more believable when you do know what you are talking about or know what you are doing.

It's also respectable to admit when you simply don't know something being asked of you and that you'll find the answers and get back to them.

Another consideration for earning influence in the eyes of others is how abundantly you place their interests above your own. Helping others be successful has a boomerang effect.

Pour kindness and belief into others and grow together. Being authentic and nurturing relationships goes a long way in preventing problems and creating opportunities. Keep in mind that genuine kindness is exclusive of practicality. Be selfless.

> *Genuine kindness is exclusive of practicality. Be selfless.*

Another facet of prevention I feel compelled to address is for those entering the workforce and what we call "the real world." This is also for my fellow college parents. It's about the importance for students to take charge of their career and life destiny and succeed despite the huge blind spots of our education experience. This is a core life priority that's close to my heart and for which I've worked extremely hard for many years to have the insight and expertise to help others.

There are some essential points to put this topic into context. The first is how high schools put students at a disadvantage because their education focuses on teaching how to test well. This is not to overlook the importance of having good grades to get into college. By and large, K-12 schools also do not sufficiently expose students to career pathways or provide enough practical training to succeed in the workplace nor do they build the life skills to become self-sufficient.

For the increasingly few who make it to college, they're still conditioned to focus on their G.P.A. instead of switch gears to acquire employable skills. Don't get me wrong, getting good grades still matters. However, today's college education typically remains exclusively academic and neglects experiential learning. In other words, no one is making students get the work and life experience to develop practical skills, such as: interpersonal communication, productivity, professionalism, critical thinking and emotional intelligence.

The point is that students come out of high school without fully understanding their options to choose a job or career, without an accurate measure of their work skills and aptitudes and without adequate personal reflection to align potential interests with life pursuits. Many of them then go through college with a limited sense of direction and exposure to their potential field of choice only to then graduate without landing on their feet or ever using their six-figure degree for which they incur decades of debt.

Now that that's out of my system, I admit to having some hard-earned concerns. I do a fair amount of speaking about related topics and often ask professionals how many of them *ever* used their college degree and, among those, who still do. Though I can't claim this to be formal research, it's been consistent. At most, 25 percent have ever used their degree and no more than 15 percent still do. There's a hidden epidemic.

INTERNING

I think you'll agree that these are incredibly significant issues in terms of most people's quality of life. In this case, prevention is about bucking the system by taking charge as early and as often as possible to get and stay on the right track. As you might expect, we'll go with the example of finding the right internship to make yourself more employable or to secure the ideal job to provide for your family. This too is a process that's often fraught with randomness. Most colleges do not provide internship "placements" and many people find a job search to be like grasping at straws.

> *The stakes are too high to be idle. There are little known, practical techniques one can follow that enable them to take charge of their career and life destiny.*

The stakes are too high to be idle. There are little-known, practical techniques one can follow that enable them to take charge of their career and life destiny. Then they must do what's necessary. This approach draws upon my professional experience and, among all else in *Z-isms,* is a free resource that I developed under the non-profit that can help millions of people, employers and employees time and time again.

In brief, StudentSTEPS.org follows four seamless steps to help someone get from being lost to arriving where they belong. It starts with using LinkedIn for targeted introductions to request informational interviews, which are the springboard that can open multiple doors of opportunity. For students, that leads to internships in which they can prove themselves, earn trust and eventually secure a job offer.

This technique follows a similar pattern for new graduates and more experienced job seekers. There's also a similar site at VETsteps.org with resources, tools and various training that are exclusive for veterans. Again, the key is that every step is in an individual's control. Have at it, go for it and manifest your desired accomplishment!

> *It's within our personal control to take charge of your career and job pathways.*

Whether you're in transition to or from college, from active duty or otherwise, it is hope-instilling to know that it's within our personal control to take charge of your career and job pathways. Relevant enough to say, applying this level of prevention will go a long way to avoid the life-long impact of blinking and having 10 or 50 years go by in some job or career that diminishes your professional satisfaction and human potential.

Well that got rather intense. The good news about being however far along in life than at the start of one's work life is that, no matter however much anyone isn't where they belong, it's never too late to change course. More evident about the ripple effect when changing occupations, is that it takes at least an equal factor and combination of high-risk tolerance, understandable trepidation and summoned bravery to see it through.

It's a relief to know we're not always entirely helpless to influence the all-important outcomes and related life experiences when it comes to certain big decisions, events and transitions.

Just to round things out, there's a very timely, major life transition I'm currently experiencing with my son Jake heading off to college. All those years of parental guidance and preventative measures, mostly as a single dad – from baby-proofing to navigating the teens

– are all behind me. We've reached the point where my parental discretion is less advised, which means it's time to relinquish some of my role to positively affect Jake's life and well-being. Suddenly, it seems there's a lot less I can prevent along with some pride and relief that some things are no longer in my hands.

Naturally, as Jake headed off to school, I didn't pass up the opportunity to convey some parting words of advice to my son. It's my right, right? I mean we're talking about putting however many preventative measures into place. I still want to have his back as he leaves the cocoon. It's also important to take some precautionary measures knowing that the rest of the world is ready for him to be fully engaged in it.

I followed through this time by leaving a letter behind knowing that my ability and influence to proactively shape his life is however less. With no further ado, below is my personal letter to Jake – verbatim – presented on the day his mom and I dropped him off and finished setting up his dorm room. This disclosure being more than my own, I do have Jake's approval to share herein:

Jaker! Miss me yet? Ok, grant me some parting advice.

1. **Turn the Page:** This is the beginning of one of your life's greatest chapters. Whatever hang-ups you have about the past, leave them behind. If you change nothing, then nothing can change. Reinvent yourself. Seriously Jake, you deserve it. Believe that and just let go.

2. **Treat Yourself Right:** Be kind. Whenever you get those thoughts running through your head that put yourself down or self-doubts, take charge and tell them to piss off. In kind, you'll also have a lot to feel good about – focus on being proud of yourself and grateful overall. I know you find this especially hard; all-the-more reason to fight back and be your own admirer.

3. **Expect the Best:** Decide what you want and go for it. Whatever you let [or make] yourself expect to happen is that much more

likely to follow suit. You'll need to work at this just the same as hitting the gym, maybe even harder. Working out will help a lot with this too. I only want the best for you and to make the most of your college days – but that's still up to you.

4. **Force Yourself into Your Discomfort Zone:** Now's your chance. Get out of your room. Join some clubs you like and some that stretch you. Besides any sports, consider checking out ones like Sports Nutrition, Athletic Training or even Photography. Whatever it is, meet more people. If you don't like a club or whatever, then you'll know it's not for you.

5. **Choose Your Tribe Well:** No need to rush or be overeager. Aside from clubs, do whatever it takes to get to know a lot of people, *especially* in the first 2-3 weeks. Spread yourself around with multiple groups instead of sticking with too small of a "Pack" too soon. [Dorm roommate's 1st name] seems like a good start. Let others be a good influence on you and, in kind, be a good influence and true friend. There's no need to force it or try too hard. Just be yourself. Listen more than you talk. You are the average sum of your five closest friends. You have 17,000+ options.

6. **Play Hard to Get:** Resist the temptation to commit to joining a fraternity, no matter how much peer pressure. Keep your options open, incl. not to join one at all. I'm sorry but the "brothers" thing is overrated. It also cuts you off from other friendships AND relationships. A lot of girls won't date "frat guys" because they don't want to label themselves. You also attach yourself to some knuckleheads wearing the same letters.

   There's a way to be a chameleon, make friends with those in multiple orgs and keep your options open. Maybe decide mid-Sophomore year. Be hard to get but not be gotten. The answer in the meantime is, "I'm not sure it's for me, at least not yet."

7. **Play it Cool:** Meet girls, but don't get a rep. It's still a small school. It will be great to meet someone you really like, but don't lose yourself in them. Be your own man.

8. **Don't be 'That Guy':** Have fun, but you don't need to win a competition to obliterate yourself and be the biggest clown in the room. You can gain more respect and a good rep in other ways. Make good decisions.

9. **Find Your Groove:** Aside from classes, create and stick to a routine. Set your alarm and other alerts. Use up your meal plan. Commit to workouts. Stay in motion.

10. **Obligatory Academic Comments:** Do your best – school comes first. Stay in touch with your advisor. Talk to students in majors that interest you. Get to know and rely on your professors.

11. **Stay in Touch:** Along with your life entering a new phase, so is our relationship. Whenever we make time to connect, let's make it count. It would be great for us to really enjoy sharing about one another's adventures and stay connected. I am always here to listen and never too far away to be there for you. *I love you more than words can express.* Dad

> *The challenge with highlighting everything is that it highlights nothing.*

If you have yet to figure it out, I do have a few soft spots. That letter covers a lot of ground. The challenge with highlighting everything is that it highlights nothing. If there's any central point I continue to reinforce it's to "make good choices," which is said half-kidding without kidding. That's the mantra I hope can be a stopgap measure in the moments it matters most, if you know what I mean. I'm always open to more advice from my fellow college parents.

While on the subject, it's not beyond me to hold up the mirror and look back at myself just the same. What are the preventative measures I missed realizing? In other words, what could I have done better raising my son? Well, parents, here's what I think it is: whenever they ask for your help, ask yourself whether they're capable of figuring it out. Then follow through by telling them to go figure things out for themselves instead. It's crucial to know when to do a little less or not make things too easy for our kids. What they need are the life skills and self-reliance to thrive without parents.

> *It's crucial to know when to do a little less or not make things too easy for our kids.*

When I went back to see this letter to share it in the book, it had only been a few months but seemed much longer. It was all-too-easy to notice that I'd never gone anywhere near this long without seeing and hanging out with my son. At the same time, we've stayed connected and I know that he's not completely gone from the nest, at least not yet. But I recognize that much of what happens now will shape our future father-son relationship.

With Jake less in the picture, I still have my share of fun with Erica and Greta. I do what I can to be the best dad and husband, including when it comes to looking out for them. It's safe to say that I do rely on certain prevention measures and influence to keep them out of trouble and/or at least save them and myself some of the trouble.

This all has less to do with being controlling, or anything, as much as it does about what I assume to be my roles and responsibilities in life, including to apply some preventive measures for the greater good, not the least of which, in this case, being my own. Anticipating, mitigating and minimizing unwanted events takes a certain degree of proactive planning and precaution.

Just remember to proceed at your own risk.

CHAPTER FOUR

Perception Is

Perception is a funny thing. Well, not always. One might say it plays tricks on you, as if "it" was some external entity rather than something within yourself. It may be more accurate to say that we play tricks on *ourselves*. Whatever our view of any event or circumstance, we assume that view is the truth when it is only an interpretation.

Perception
(Noun) [per-sep-sh*uh*n]

> *A single unified awareness derived from sensory processes while a stimulus is present as interpreted with the mind; cognition; understanding.*

Without realizing it, we isolate a set of what we consider facts and create stories around them as if they are the whole truth. Just because something feels real does not make it true and the meaning that we assign can be very subjective, judgmental and completely inaccurate.

> **Just because something feels real does not make it true.**

It's essential to contemplate how we can see things so differently within ourselves and understand that that perception can and will be altered by various stimuli. Consider the even greater variable of how two or more people perceive the very same events. It gives new meaning to the old adage of there being at least three sides to every circumstance - person A's side, person B's side, and the truth.

Most of us are familiar with the expression of seeing the world through rose-colored glasses. Here we view a certain set of circumstances in a generally positive way that fuels our happiness and contentment.

In contrast, either you or anyone with whom you interact can take the very same set of circumstances viewed through a lens of optimism and have a completely opposite perception than someone who sees through one of pessimism. Both individuals perceive those same circumstances much differently.

There's a good reason why the saying about a glass being half full or empty continues to stand the test of time. It's important to challenge and remind yourself to find the most optimistic vantage point by applying your Earned Confidence. Be willing to turn the kaleidoscope and look again. Find the shape that looks the least distorted.

Objectivity
(Noun) [ob-jik-tiv-i-tee]

> *Expressing or dealing with facts or conditions as perceived without distortion by personal feelings, prejudices, or interpretations as if external to the mind.*

The landscape here is multi-dimensional and varies by individual. As a result, it would be easy to spiral into the land of confusion.

Let's not go there. More to the point is that people always have unique circumstances with many moving parts. They possess different values, character traits and perspectives, such as happiness among all else.

Drilling down even further is how we define our values and what shapes them based on how well we truly know ourselves. Who we are and how we perceive ourselves is colored by society, the media and our professional world while being influenced by expectations from our spouse, partners, family and friends. It can be difficult to differentiate and determine which values are yours and which belong to outside influences.

If this hits home, then it makes sense to take the time and make an effort to pinpoint what is most important to you. What instills you with the most joy? What are your dreams and desires?

What instills you with the most joy?

What are your dreams and desires?

You may also find it beneficial to identify the things you don't like or even hate, as well as what fears may shape your perspective. These, too, add complexities to how we perceive others and the world around us.

There are a vast number of sources and tools to help guide and refine this self-discovery. You are the last person to be shy about. Just go for it as if you were learning about someone new you find exciting or interesting. Scratch that. Consider yourself to be exciting and interesting!

There's also an abundance of research available if you'd like to go deeper. This is not the book for finding scientific studies. Not being boring seems like a good approach! There was a very cool one I found that, "Open-minded people have a different visual perception of reality." It explains how the 'gate' that lets information through to our consciousness may have a different level of flexibility and that open people appear to have a more flexible gate than the average person. Wasn't that riveting?!

Okay, now you know why that's the only citation of formal research you'll have to endure.

Moving on, another aspect worth considering relates to our values and how each of us prioritize certain "life currencies" differently. Examples include: the importance of good health, love, family, friendships, energy, time and freedom, just to name a few.

We must also be realistic about the fact that perception has a lot to do with life circumstances, specific events and any number of factors within and outside of our control. Yet they affect us nonetheless. Of course, one of the most obvious factors is one's perspective about their economic circumstances.

Financial wherewithal is what most people think of when they hear "currency" and it can matter quite a bit. Then again, at this very moment, it' seems certain that there are the poorest of children in some third world country playing in rubble and having the time of their lives. There are also any number of exceptionally wealthy people in the world who exist in the category of the most miserable human beings on the planet. Happiness, as you can see, is somewhat relative.

The other currency less obvious to those in good health is most obvious to those who must contend with any physical or mental disabilities that diminish their quality of life in relation to the extent of such afflictions.

That said, when it comes to our priorities about life currencies relative to our values, let's approach this topic based on the assumption that we are in reasonably good health and have some level of stability in our financial conditions. Both of those concerns can drastically affect one's outlook and perceptions.

This is in no way to slight a significant majority of the U.S. population or anyone anywhere else who live paycheck to paycheck, or experience greater financial distress.

For me, beyond essential needs, the life currency that matters most is not time or energy management, it's about freedom. This is what has made it possible for me to bring the book to fruition. It's also why I pushed myself in 2002 to start my first company and have fought tooth and nail to keep the freedom to make my own schedule. It takes a greater risk-threshold but it's entirely worth the sacrifices and trade-offs, at least for me.

> *The life currency that matters most is not time or energy management, it's about freedom.*

In those years, as my own nest egg was exhausting came my father's passing and the resulting inheritance. That paid for all the training materials and intellectual property that I developed under The Internship Institute and Z University. In that way, my parents were my Angel Investors but they only got me so far. Over the years, I've been awarded several federal and state workforce grants totaling $845,000. That may sound like a lot but grants are unforgiving in that I never saw most of that funding, including much of which was to pay interns.

You do what it takes. Along the way, all the things that make up our perceptions of such events can represent very different perspectives of the truth. It's ultimately up to us to make those choices and navigate accordingly.

Overall, as our priorities about life currencies align with our values, we recognize how these also add a means through which we see and interpret each of our experiences.

As we take a closer look at the "he said, she said" scenario between persons A and B, it's essential to consider factors like our interpersonal communication skills and ability to express ourselves fully. Are we quiet and reserved? Do we fear judgment or rejection? Maybe we default to aggression and fail to hear others out. Coping skills, such as patience and poise, also come into play.

In the context of the more technical Sender-Receiver Model of communication, what level of active listening does the receiver exert versus being someone with selective hearing? This falls among what we just covered about assumptive thinking. When possible, start with a baseline of the known truth about when, where, how and who.

We also alter our perceptions all the time, which may be in relation to our actual mood or level of fatigue. When our wagon is dragging, we might turn to caffeine. If we feel a little down, we may listen to our favorite music to get a needed boost. A decision to consume alcohol or other mind-altering substances is also one to change perception. That covers that.

> *In much the same way as working out, certain behaviors and practices are like building a muscle.*

Another option to consider is journaling, which can lend a different perspective about your relationship with yourself and how you view things upon that self-reflection. In much the same way as with working out, certain behaviors and practices are like building a muscle. If you've never journaled, then try getting out of your own way and see how it goes. The benefits may surprise you. There's also the importance of hitting the gym and other ways to nurture the mind and body as a healthy means to reset how we interpret the world around us. We'll get more into that soon.

We're also about to discuss how having one's mood exceed the normal range, such as with clinical depression or anxiety, is another factor. Of course, someone's perception filter can vary based on their mood or emotional level at any point, on any given day and during any circumstance. In the obvious example of an argument, with emotions running high, it can be more difficult to rationalize something with someone in less than a rational state of mind. The rest goes without saying.

Among the most common ways perception varies is how we experience time. We sometimes refer to certain hours, days, weeks, months, seasons or years as "flying by." My son just started college. Where did the time go? Yet we get to experience the likes of waiting lines, traffic and trips to the dentist as taking forever. Obviously, time is a precise constant and a very straightforward point for us to contemplate here.

One aspect worth delving into further is encouraging yourself to heighten your mindful awareness by taking opportunities to live in the current moment. What's the slowest you can perceive time?

Take just five minutes. Observe how a breeze passes through a tall tree. Watch a cloud change shape. Chew slower and relish your taste buds. Experience the water hit and roll off your body in the shower. Study your child's facial expressions. Interact with your pet. Even the one-minute gratitude exercise we'll discuss later will seem much longer. See if you can feel a palpable shift of reality, if even for a few minutes.

Many of us get uncomfortable when these simple exercises begin to feel too long. We get impatient with ourselves and gravitate back to experiencing life at full speed. Explore this further.

Block out 5 minutes and pick 5 different things on which to narrow your focus and perception.

You are hereby challenged to try this for five days. Set a reminder on your phone. Block out a whole 5 minutes and pick 5 different things on which to narrow your focus and perception. Consider writing down the self-observations specific to your experiences about how you felt doing it as opposed to observations about what you were observing. Did you get more comfortable with yourself each time? Will you find that this exercise gets easier and that you are more at ease by Day 5? This is analogous to practicing meditation.

Objectively, knowing that our time on this Earth is finite, it stands to reason that we'd appreciate life considerably more to whatever degree we can slow down our perception of time and do our best to enjoy the moment. It's a powerful practice to experience gratitude and another sound justification to be in the now.

I started college as an aspiring filmmaker and my first class was all about aesthetics. My professor was this seemingly erratic, artsy egomaniac who wore a French beret to stand in front of

300 freshman and pontificate about the interpretation of beauty. He asked us all, "What is beauty?" Here's where we might think of being in nature or touring a museum. It's also that territory of perception in which what we interpret is purely in the eye of the beholder. Of course, I've yet to become that filmmaker, which is another story.

There's no doubt that we could highlight any number of other variables that color our perceptions but the ones we have already covered are enough to allow us to see plainly why it is so easy to misinterpret others' messages and miscommunicate our ideas and sentiments. Seek objectivity.

Of course, the most obvious influences on our perceptions involve the five senses and their variable mix in affecting our individual receptors. Is seeing believing?

Our brains receive and interpret a constant flow of information.

That's a timely question, so let's explore that for a moment. Our brains receive and interpret a constant flow of information. Sight, touch and hearing are our primary windows that allow us to perceive the world, interpret our environment and interact with others.

Naturally each of us has a dominant sense that drives what and how we interpret our surroundings. Which is yours? You probably know. One way to be surer is whether you and others consider you to be a good listener. Otherwise, you're probably more sight-dominant.

This can be even more essential when it comes to interpersonal communication and knowing about how others interpret information as well as how they express themselves. You can look for indicators such as language cues. Are they more inclined to say, "I see what you're saying" or "I hear what you're saying?"

Knowing this about yourself, along with harnessing your powers of observation, are critical skills to help you improve the accuracy of your perceptions. While we're at it, let's factor in your and their mood and energy at a given moment and how those influence corresponding speech, tone, facial expressions and eye contact as our "windows to the soul." Wait, we almost forgot body language. Have you heard the one about how it may be as much as 90 percent of communication? Do you believe that? I'm not so sure.

> *It's a fair assumption that much of what we encounter is imperceptible.*

In light of these multi-sensory facets, it's a fair assumption that much of what we encounter is imperceptible. At the very least, it stands to reason that our perceptions have their limits, which is also a good reason to give others the benefit of the doubt.

We seem to have given this topic its due, so let's move on before we end up with another book within the book.

Here's a personal favorite example about perception that might just make you think at least twice. This may sound more like a joke at first, but it's not. Picture this:

There are three travelers who need a place to stay for the night. They find an inn where they're told the room is $30.00. Easy enough, they each chip in a $10.00 bill and they go about their business to their room.

Soon after, the innkeeper realizes he overcharged them by $5.00. He calls the bellhop, hands him five $1.00 bills from the cash register and asks him to deliver the refund.

Instead, the bellhop decides to pocket $2.00 as a gratuity and figures the travelers will be none the wiser.

Wrapping this up, he knocks on their door and, to their satisfaction, hands them the remaining $3.00, which naturally splits perfectly 3 ways. It seems very simple and straightforward. Each traveler paid a $10.00 bill and received a $1.00 bill in return. They each paid $9.00 for the room. It's even money, right?

Well, if $9.00 x 3 travelers equals $27.00 and the bellhop pocketed $2.00, that only adds up to $29.00. What happened to the missing dollar? It seems like basic math. We can even go back over it, lay out actual currency to recount and yet it still comes up short. What happened? Magic? Some sort of anomaly? We'll revisit this later.

> *Consider what else we perceive less than wholly accurate.*

Math is supposed to be precise. Not this time. Something is off. It seems to defy logic to be anything but the exact truth. Did we allow false confidence to fool ourselves that we followed every detail? It's a lot like losing a shell game. We perceive something as seeming perfectly accurate but the answer is lost somewhere in translation. If we can lose track of that dollar so quickly, consider what else we perceive less than wholly accurate.

There's also the question of what it takes to adapt our perceptions when our five senses encounter deprivation or disorientation. The example that comes to mind has to do with a unique experience in my early teens that is among the highlights of my life which occurred at a hockey camp in Northern Ontario. It regards a precise technique done by water-skiers called a "Deep Water Barefoot Start."

This is when a skier has no skis. It's just them, the handled rope, the speedboat, the driver and the second person in the boat known as the "Spotter." In short, it's as close as one can get to being a human torpedo.

For the purposes of describing this barefooting challenge, try to follow these details and imagine as if it were you instead. Are you ready?

First off, performing this maneuver requires the skier to have a smooth body surface, so you need a very tight wetsuit that can squeeze *over* a lifejacket and still zip. How does that feel?! You may find it a little hard to breathe at first.

Snap, we're in the water and ready to go. The maneuver begins by crossing one's feet on the rope and holding on as tight as possible. Then, while leaning back, you shout to alert the boat driver that you're ready for them to hit the throttle. The next 8 to 12 seconds are most simply described as having a unique experience and sensations.

Aside from holding on tight and making your body rigid to maintain position, the most critical aspect is to throw and keep your head all the way back so your chin creates an air pocket while torpedoing and prevents you from choking on a rush of water going up your nose. This position also secures the rope from jolting through and scarring your legs. You've got a lot on your mind.

From there is a sequence of several more technical maneuvers to do while the boat reaches barefoot speed. This is calculated by dividing one's body weight by 10 and adding 20 to 25 mph. Hold your position!

You've just torpedoed and are now bouncing around and experiencing more disorientation.

Here's the point of the story. When the boat reaches that barefoot speed, the Spotter signals the skier so they know it's time to plant their feet. The challenge at this point is that you've just torpedoed and are now bouncing around and experiencing more disorientation. Yet you must maintain concentration to complete the maneuver.

As you can imagine, planting the feet from a horizontal position with the water surface creates a tremendous amount of spray at that high speed. There's a moment of total confusion. In fact, the sensation is so disorienting that it causes the skier to think that they've wiped out. Their reflex is to let go of the rope to avoid being dragged by the boat. So, what did I do? That's right. I let go.

The reality is that everything was fine. The Spotter called out to confirm "you had it." So we had to do the whole sequence all over again. Sure enough, when I planted my feet that next time, I experienced the same disorientation and had the same reflex.

We then got to the third attempt and it was clear that this was my last one for the day. Aside from the boat waves disrupting the glassy lake, it takes a lot out of you and I was getting tired. Sure enough, this time I decided to focus on my training in "dry land practice," especially to square up my feet and ignore what my brain was telling me.

Finally came the sensation I'd yet to have. Once I fought through the reflex and just held on to get into the standing position, the spray began to fade away until it all flowed behind me. Everything became completely clear and I started yelling to celebrate.

Just believe in yourself and hold on tight until everything clears.

In the end, what I learned and want to share with you is that: when your senses are disoriented or your perception is challenged all you have to do is rely on yourself and trust the process. Just believe in yourself and hold on tight until everything clears. You'll soon realize that you're on the other side and know that you're still standing!

As a brief aside, this led to an even more meaningful experience a short time later when I teamed up with two instructors to perform a barefoot pyramid. Any guess how fast we were going? The math is the same.

I occasionally revisit this moment in my life, which has less to do with the experience itself as much as it does with reconnecting with my inner kid and his sense of life and excitement.

Back then, he was much more confident on ice and water than on land.

Seeing my fist in the air, I will always remember that feeling of triumph. My facial expression also holds greater meaning because we had to fail quite a few times before we were able to stand on six feet.

> *Seeing my fist in the air, I will always remember that feeling of triumph.*

Can you think of certain photos that capture such moments in your life that help you revisit and reconnect with your identity? It's a positive way to soul search and stay true to yourself. It's also a good way to ground your self-perceptions.

Whether you're relying on external or internal perceptions, be open to the possibilities of them being skewed for any number of reasons. Be more objective about your true self, others and the events you encounter.

Start by asking yourself a simple question: How's life?

Then, take stock.

On second thought, let's get into action. How full is your glass?

As discussed at the beginning of the chapter, we can perceive the same set of life circumstances very differently on any given day. As hard as we may try to align our perceptions with reality, it's worth considering the extent to which they're already one in the same.

One obvious factor is our actual situation. Most of us are always going through something to whatever degree. Personality traits, behaviors and our disposition surely play a major role. We've all heard and have hopefully experienced good things about the power of positive thinking.

Another major consideration is our state of mood health. Could our brain chemistry be the biggest difference in how we perceive the world around us? The best time for that question may be on a day when you're feeling a bit down and are able to rally yourself to exercise. Then compare notes.

Here's a simple way to do just that. Take a Perception Snapshot with the grid below. Feel free to alter it to align with your own life priorities. Then simply go down the list and decide whether to mark each with a plus or minus sign. Hopefully you can maintain and feel good about having your basic needs met and that all your loved ones remain healthy.

Perception Snapshot

LIFE PRIORITIES	POSITIVE (+)	NEGATIVE (-)
Basic Needs Met	+	
Personal Health	+	
Romance		−
Family/Kids		−
Friends	+	
Finances	+	
The Job		−
Boss/Coworkers		−
Work-Life Balance	+	

Go a step further and allow yourself to feel as grateful as possible for everything you decide is going well. Few of us are without our share of minus signs. What actions can you take to change your answers for the better? Could it be as simple as making a conscious decision to shift your perceptions?

Are these things really all that bad? You might find it helpful to rate and rank each one. Can you see some light at the end of the tunnel? Is it an accurate statement to say that this too shall pass? If certain stressors truly are what they are, to what degree can you improve your coping skills?

Take heart. Today will be soon be in your review mirror. Tomorrow can bring a fresh start.

Put your mind to it and see what happens.

CHAPTER FIVE

Minding the Mood Scale

Okay, the mental health topic has come up multiple times. Let's take it head on instead of tap-dancing around it.

First, a private disclosure: I am among those who have had to battle depression. This is something I've kept to myself all my life. Depression has had its way with me numerous times since my early teens. While it's evident that I'm not a clinician, there's something to be said for the credibility of speaking from experience. Most treatment providers are only capable of taking an academic approach with an uncertain degree of disconnection.

Fortunately, it's been a number of years since I've had a major bout. If you've never had the misfortune of being in the grips of severe depression and the depths of despair, consider yourself lucky.

We've already covered this topic in relation to it diminishing accurate perception and Earned Confidence. As we explore further, it's important to distinguish that this is less about perceiving and dealing with external circumstances as much as it's about its impact turned inward.

Everyone can self-identify as having a certain range of the happiness and sadness they experience. Then there are some who must contend with increased instability in either direction, the more typical one being downward.

> *There's just
> no other way
> but through.*

It's also natural for people to dip or rise beyond the normal range, especially with the many challenging life events everyone inevitably encounters. Summoning ones' Earned Confidence can only get them so far when they are fully in the thick of things emotionally. Coping healthily with such events includes feeling the pain that comes with them. There is just no other way but through. Making time and space to feel true sadness is important. Being overcome by it is something else entirely.

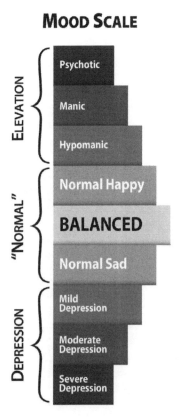

MOOD SCALE

ELEVATION
- Psychotic
- Manic
- Hypomanic

"NORMAL"
- Normal Happy
- **BALANCED**
- Normal Sad

DEPRESSION
- Mild Depression
- Moderate Depression
- Severe Depression

With that in mind, it's a reasonable assumption that just about everyone knows what it's like to experience some level of clinical depression. Similarly, if you think of the times in your life that brought you somewhere in the vicinity of Cloud Nine, that will give you a sense of the minor elevation referred to as hypomania.

Delving further into this topic, we can illustrate these experiences as occurring along a Mood Scale that works much like a thermometer.

This illustration is not a static drawing. Everyone is different. For discussion purposes, let's agree that the middle section represents the normal range and not debate who gets to define what is clinically accurate or socially acceptable. Instead, let's focus on the unhealthy part of Mental Health: the aspect that extends further above or below the normal range on the Mood Scale for a sustained period and legitimately may be defined as experiencing mental imbalance.

This is where we are no longer in the category of excessive happiness or sadness in which normal, healthy individuals possess the elasticity to bounce back. This is more in the realm of physical brain chemistry. However temporary or persistent this impairment, we can classify this as being sick in much the same way as one might catch a cold in mild cases or have the flu or pneumonia in moderate or more severe cases, respectively.

People elevating into a hypomanic state present a greater danger to themselves or others and exhibit increasingly erratic behavior, among other symptoms.

> *Keeping up with life's demands feels more like wading through quicksand.*

In contrast, depression poses a much greater threat when it reaches a moderate level with the sufferer no longer able to pull out of it. The person may find keeping up with life's demands feels more like wading through quicksand. The deeper the depression, the further they sink and the harder it becomes to escape.

The true insidiousness of this affliction, especially at the lower level, is that depression is almost indiscernible to the sufferer, let alone observers. It can be as subtle as a persistent lack of motivation to do basic tasks. It may be that you are falling behind on things and are unsure why. Depression creeps up on you. It physically sabotages your brain and impedes you from living life to the fullest.

It's not until you lift out of that funk that you realize you have been out of touch with feeling like yourself and that you have been depressed all along. This is often after extended periods of time. Doing too much of the same thing as a distraction, especially TV and video games, is both symptomatic and exacerbating.

Nothing against binge-watching our favorite shows, but one binge after another can turn a few days into weeks and even months.

It's essential to take a dose of prevention or, at the very least, avert things from worsening. Those at risk can rely on the 3-Day Rule. We all have down days. Two in a row is a red flag. When there's three days in a row, it's time to take action. This applies to everyone, including if you consider your mood range to be normal. There are some non-pharmaceutical remedies we can rely on when we observe ourselves or those close to us to be clinically depressed or experience a mood elevation above the normal range.

First and foremost is to get to the gym. You heard me. Physical exercise is, by far, the single most beneficial action anyone can take to get their head straight. So dust off the stationary bike or dig your gym membership card out of the bottom of your drawer. Just take better care of yourself. Get enough sleep, eat well and insulate yourself from stress. Make it a routine instead of something reactive to feeling less than normal – whatever you consider that to be. Rely on the Self-Care Report Card just ahead.

The thing with the 3-Day Rule is that, for every additional day someone sinks deeper into depression or elevates, it may take two more days to rebound. Of course, this is not a hard and fast rule. The same may be said for those who are "rapid cyclers," which mainly applies to those who contend with bipolar or manic-depressive disorder.

What do you know you need to do and not give yourself the option to not do?

That said, if you don't quite feel like yourself, be open to the possibility that it's not your fault. Simply take the necessary actions to self-correct. If there was ever a case of something being easier said than done, this is that challenge. You might have to roleplay in being your own rescuer to pull yourself through and out of the quicksand. What do you know you need to do and not give yourself the option to not do? Start there.

Confide in a trusted friend to be your accountability partner. Get into some sort of daily physical routine, be it to take a walk or some other activities that get you or your loved ones out of the house. Overall, aside from the core benefit of physical activity, the ultimate key is to have structure and then force yourself to stick to that plan knowing you probably won't feel like it.

Given that we're addressing a specific medical affliction, this is where my expertise wanes. Obviously, I am not a doctor, so let's turn to the experts. The Mayo Clinic specifies the clinical description of depression as follows:

> *A major depressive episode includes symptoms that are severe enough to cause noticeable difficulty in day-to-day activities, such as work, school, social activities or relationships. An episode includes five or more of these symptoms:*
>
> * *Depressed mood, such as feeling sad, empty, hopeless or tearful (in children and teens, depressed mood can appear as irritability)*
> * *Marked loss of interest or feeling no pleasure in all – or almost all – activities*
> * *Significant weight loss when not dieting, weight gain, or decrease or increase in appetite (in children, failure to gain weight as expected can be a sign of depression)*
> * *Insomnia or sleeping too much*
> * *Restlessness or slowed behavior*
> * *Fatigue or loss of energy*
> * *Feelings of worthlessness and excessive or inappropriate guilt*
> * *Decreased ability to think or concentrate; indecisiveness*
> * *Thinking about, planning or attempting suicide*

Speaking to depression with more familiarity, you may find that you are increasingly verbally abusive to yourself and begin to accept those criticisms and feelings as absolutes. For instance, that might sound like, "I will never be happy again."

This is about when the experience of self-abuse being described here is correctly symptomatic of clinical depression. This brings us back to the implied fact that each of us are the only ones who truly know what we are experiencing. Low levels of depression or anxiety may also be a natural experience rather than an imbalance warranting medication to correct that brain chemistry.

It was nearly 20 years ago when someone I trust and who knows me well said something that helped get me through the despair of deeper depression. They pointed out that, "No matter how bad you feel or how things may seem, you will feel better at some point. Things won't always be this way." It's a real life-preserver to remind yourself or someone close enough who you know to be clinically depressed or hypomanic.

> *No matter how bad you feel, or how things may seem, you will feel better at some point.*

I saw something similar along these lines that if you rearrange the letters in the word depression you'll get, "I pressed on." Your current situation is not your destination.

It's very difficult to see how darkly your depressed perceptions color your world.

If you ever find yourself unable to rebound or feel like you're in a freefall and sinking lower, then I implore and encourage you to seek help. This also certainly applies to helping someone else in need.

It may be a matter of medication being a partial solution but do not wait and prolong unnecessary suffering. A critical note here is that, often it is very difficult to schedule psychiatric appointments quickly or frequently enough. Fortunately, telehealth services are now more accessible for anyone to get a professional evaluation.

If warranted, put any hang-ups aside and check yourself into a *reputable* in-patient facility or some other higher level of care where medical professionals are readily available to closely monitor medications and mood stability. This may be the best course of action to rebalance your brain chemistry and restore physical health in the shortest amount of time so that you can return to your true self. Here's when to remind yourself, again, by calling upon your Earned Confidence to realize and expect that brighter days lie ahead.

Remember that some people aren't as fortunate to find the right medication the first time. No one said that remedying one's mood balance was a walk in the park. It's also no picnic with the side effects people suffer.

It takes time to find the right medication to balance your mood impairment, let alone at the right dose to be administered the right way.

Do whatever it takes. If you find that is the case personally, then patience, persistence and self-compassion are vital to your core health.

I believe the physical affliction at the root of abnormal mental health relates to the speed of how slowly or rapidly one's synapses fire, which is the function of brain chemicals, most notably Serotonin and Dopamine.

What's important to keep in mind about the Mood Scale is how it corresponds with feelings and actions you and others experience progressively. If others close to you observe a change in behavior, be it a downward spiral or increasing hyperactivity, then you or that person need a confidante. Speaking with someone you trust or being there for someone else, gives you or that person a safety net.

Can you see yourself on this scale? Does this resonate with you? Seriously, who gets to define normalcy and the Happy-Sad range as being clinically healthy versus there being a physical chemical imbalance that potentially requires greater intervention? That is one role of mental health professionals but you must still trust yourself.

This brings us back to our Earned Confidence. When I experience sadness, especially what I know to be in the normal range, I gravitate toward optimism and do a check-in with myself. I'm even more in favor of the 2-Day Rule. Personally, I'm a slow mover on the Mood Scale. But there's still a distinct progression that, if unchecked, could lead to a clinically legitimate mental health event.

We also need to take a closer look at symptoms of mood elevation, those being manic impulses, behaviors and successively something more overt. In contrast to how depression creeps up on you and stays under the surface for prolonged periods, manic behavior is exponentially obvious and often worsens rapidly. Left unchecked, it becomes more destructive as one approaches the edge of madness.

Here's where we need another consult from our friends at the Mayo Clinic:

> *Mania and hypomania are two distinct types of episodes, but they have the same symptoms. Mania is more severe than hypomania and causes more noticeable problems at work, school, and social activities, as well as relationship difficulties. Mania may also trigger a break from reality (psychosis) and require hospitalization.*
>
> *Both a manic and a hypomanic episode include three or more of these symptoms:*
>
> - *Abnormally upbeat, jumpy or wired*
> - *Increased activity, energy or agitation*
> - *Exaggerated sense of well-being and self-confidence (euphoria)*
> - *Decreased need for sleep*
> - *Unusual talkativeness*
> - *Racing thoughts*
> - *Distractibility*
> - *Poor decision-making. For example, going on buying sprees, taking sexual risks or making foolish investments*

Many of the symptoms above are indicative of rapid synapses.

They overwhelm and wear down brain function. It can be tempting to hold onto euphoric feelings but they become increasingly unstable and unsustainable.

If you or someone close to you is in trouble or headed for it, please take charge and seek help for everyone's benefit. Therapy is a sensible choice. However, for an actual chemical imbalance, especially with manic elevation, medication may be the only intervention and course to restore well-being.

Now to the indignities of our society. No matter how much stigmas dissipate and science advances, there is no shame in taking the best care of yourself. It is no different than having to stay on medication for a thyroid disorder or keeping cholesterol in check.

> *Few of us are without a family member or close friend who've faced a mental health event.*

Few of us are without a family member or close friend who've faced a mental health event at some point. Hopefully, it was not the ultimate event that left others with so many questions and inexplicable grief.

Who among us has had to contend with a mental imbalance or break from reality at some point in their lifetime? It runs in almost everyone's family, whether overtly or not.

Personally, I did not exactly inherit the best gene pool. My Dad (1931-2006) was bipolar. My Mom (1935-1996) suffered terribly from depression for most of her young life, including being a suicide survivor. Sadly, my brother David (1963-2012) eventually succumbed to his battle. The stakes are much higher whenever suicide runs in your family.

So if you somehow perceive that we have delved more deeply than necessary into this topic, you know my personal reasons why. It's tempting to go into greater depth with stories like those shared in all other chapters. But the intent of this one is to educate and provide context while staying on track. Besides, this is a good topic to continue in private in our Reader Forum.

Although Western Culture continues to make strides, we're still nowhere close to moving beyond societal stigmas about mental health affliction. We're that much more on our own. I hope making it a priority to include this in the book does the good for which it is intended.

CHAPTER SIX

Managing Energy

By now, most of us adhere to some level of energy management and awareness. Every thought, feeling and action has an energy consequence. Energy cannot be destroyed. It can only be transferred.

Being surrounded by various activities and interacting with others affects one another.

A simple example is when you encounter a restaurant server in a bad mood.

> *Every thought, feeling and action has an energy consequence.*

Let's say you walk in with some friends and you're all smiling and laughing. Then, without warning, your server clearly flips your group an attitude for no reason.

Their negative vibe is palpable. You all take notice. In the exchange, two of your friends suddenly find themselves annoyed about the server's attitude. Everyone was in a good mood just a moment ago. What happened? It's a form of energy transference.

Alternatively, you and your other friends choose to keep your shields up, remain neutral and recognize that the person is just having a bad day. Put another way, you make a conscious choice not to let it negatively affect your good times together. You take a healthy approach to rely on a dose of compassion and remain objective.

Good vibes can be just as contagious.

You might even go a step further and make an intentional decision and effort to cheer up your server by finding a way to make them smile or even laugh. Let's say you give that a go. Giving off good vibes can be just as contagious.

My son and I often do this when we encounter someone who clearly needs a lift. We try to give them a reason to smile. It might be cracking a joke or being self-deprecating. Mainly, it's Jake making fun of me. It's a simple act of non-random kindness with near instant, all-around gratification.

Now, let's apply some energy awareness whereby you maintain that mental armor, especially in a room full of strangers, such as at a professional networking event. You stay keenly aware of what kind of mood those around you are in, as well as your own, and act carefully and respectfully. But when you let down your guard, that energy transference becomes unnoticeable and your mood shifts inexplicably. Most people remain unmindful about this phenomenon.

How about when energy exchanges in crowds, especially sporting events? We often refer to the advantage of having the home field, ice and court. Sure, there are other factors like familiarity and players not having to travel, but most of us have first-hand experience with a shift in momentum when the home team *feeds* off their fans.

Another practical application for an energy exchange involves everyday life, mainly when it comes to being with yourself. In this case, the exchange represents a form of personal currency of the amount and kinds of energy you possess.

> **Remain keenly self-aware about your energy levels.**

In the example of any given workday, remain keenly self-aware about your energy levels. It's important to know when you have reached the point of being out of gas. Maybe you catch yourself writing the same email or sentence for 10 minutes. That's a good time to make a habit of stepping away when possible. Stay in self-awareness mode. A well-established general rule is to take breaks about every 60 to 90 minutes, or less, to maintain optimal energy.

It may seem counterintuitive to stop working. That can be true when you're in a groove. For most other times, just taking a few minutes to find your reset button will boost your overall productivity.

There are also those times to check in with yourself to align your energy level with certain activities that you need to complete. If it was me in the example of struggling to write that email, I'd stop then and there to do something easier instead. It could be filing, laundry or some other mindless chore.

Repurposing myself in this way coincides with time management in that I'm still doing what needs to get done. It's just something less taxing. You don't have to work at home to find something that still needs doing.

The same goes for aligning your optimal energy with more intense activity that requires higher mental acuity. Such tasks may also be most productively accomplished by doing 15 to 20-minute "sprints" to achieve your desired results.

This is when it's best to cultivate habits in concert with behavioral "triggers" to stay on top of your awareness game and maintain your composure. This is a good point for a shout-out to Brendon Burchard for his *High Performance Habits*. He's a great champion of these techniques and practices what he preaches. That guy does his homework and turns it in!

As with many of the other topics we've covered, it takes practice and discipline to create new habits. How badly do you want your quality of life to be even the slightest bit better? What's it worth to you to change your behavior or at least improve your current habits? What are some things you can do to feel better and be your best self? Is it to lose weight, commit to a workout routine, gain more energy and/or improve your life balance, such as enjoying more family time?

One of the most basic aspects of Managing Energy is your own decision-making process, be it as routine as what to have for dinner or something major like deciding which house to buy.

I can easily look back to my younger days and recall overthinking things. Gratefully, I have experienced some life upgrades on this subject with special thanks to Malcom Gladwell for his book, *Blink*. The central point he proved is that those who make decisions by trusting their gut make as good, if not better decisions than overthinkers. That condition is better known as "analysis paralysis."

I've worked hard over the years to trust my gut more and rely on Earned Confidence to not expend unnecessary energy by overthinking or over-preparing for things. All of us are forever a work in progress.

That said, the next time you find yourself wrestling with yourself, try doing a "gut check" and just go with it!

Here's a way to stay positive, or at least neutral, with Managing Energy. It can apply to any time someone says or does something that bothers you. Your immediate impulse may be to push back and say something. This could lead to any number of different spirals, such as an argument or discussing something over and over again that leads to suffering through the resulting negativity and energy drain. Sound familiar?

Now, go back to the original comment or action. Could it have been a single occurrence? If your ultimate objective is to prevent someone from saying or doing something again, then why say anything the first time?

Think about it. By saying or doing something in response, you may very well be the actual cause of the very thing you want to prevent.

In short, as hard as it may be, wait until the second time someone says or does something you do not want them to do again. Save yourself the grief and the resulting self-inflicted wounds. Trust me, it's a real energy-saver!

The same goes for work-life balance. Ask yourself something right now:

Do I live to work, or do I work to live?

> **Do I live to work, or do I work to live?**

This can be a crucial moment to redefine your life priorities. In fact, might this be a good time to take a break from reading? A lot of us could benefit from learning the lesson that it's completely okay to take five. I won't take it personally if that's not something you want to do this very moment, in which case just pretend that you did.

In these five minutes, or whatever time you allow, there could be lots of other things that would help you relax and regain focus. It could be stretching, checking sports scores, going on a brisk walk, meditating, napping, playing a mindless game or shopping online. Some of us do more of this than others but not necessarily as an intentional habit.

On a positive note is the importance of being good to yourself. Do you treat yourself like a best friend? Be kind and give yourself a break. Are you overworking yourself? For what? Have more fun! If you want to go home and meet up with friends to share a bottle of wine or have a few beers, go for it. Live life!

The above approaches to being mindful of energy focus on what we generate and manage within ourselves. Another major part of the energy equation goes well beyond those we encounter and handle in the moment, like the moody restaurant server. This is a good time to take a fresh look at who we surround ourselves with on an ongoing basis.

For many of us, the primary source of our happiness and fulfillment is about connection and its importance to each of us as human beings. We are social creatures. Aside from our connection with others is the impact of our relationship with ourselves in being our own best friend or our own worst enemy. We'll cover more on this later.

> **We become the combined average sum of the five people we associate with most.**

I believe there's a certain truth to the thought that we become the combined average sum of the five people we associate with most. This is especially true during our years in high school and college. Though we do not get to choose our family, we do have significant control over our friendships, romantic relationships and work acquaintances. Keep in mind that we also control the amount of time and the activities we do together. So who are those five people in your life?

For purposes of this conversation, let's regard them as our "Tribe." What do the members of your Tribe typically do to contribute or take away from your happiness? If you identify one or more individuals who tend to drain your energy more than they do to feed it, it may be time to reconsider with whom you spend your time.

> **Healthy people don't go around destroying others.**

Trust your personal warning system, part of which we touched on about Spidery manipulators and when stress seeps into your sleep. Again, if you wake up in the middle of the night or first thing in the morning and a certain person or situation is inflicting involuntary stress, it's time to make that a high priority to seek relief. Remember, those who mistreat others are the ones with something wrong. Healthy people don't go around destroying others.

This is a good motive to connect with your inner Zen and make it more readily accessible when situations come up. The traditional practice, rooted in Buddhism, describes a state of calm attentiveness in which one's actions are guided by intuition rather than conscious effort. Essentially, it's to trust yourself with a grounded calm, draw upon your Earned Confidence and act with presence of mind.

This is also an ideal moment to apply the "thin-slicing" approach from Gladwell's *Blink*, which is to identify a singular data point that represents all you need to know about something or someone on which to base a decision overall.

The essential question was whether they fed or drained my energy.

Personally, having been a single dad for a number of years, I did my share of dating and have had several meaningful relationships prior to meeting Erica. Nevertheless, whenever the time came to consider the dating checklist of what mattered to me in being with someone, there was a certain checkbox that mattered most. I had to consider the essential question about the overall experience of being with that person, which was whether they boosted or drained my energy.

A subset of that was whether I felt they brought out the best in me and inspired growth or they were stifling and brought out my lesser self. Maybe any of these individuals who are truly Spiders function more like "energy vampires" in your life. This may sound harsh but it's too important to ignore.

Is someone holding you back and sapping your quality of life? Is it clear that the only behavior and perspective you're able to change is your own? Might this be the right time to recalculate your self-worth? If not now, why not and when else?

When you find yourself inexplicably coming back for more, it's akin to needing to break a bad habit. The only way to have the happiness you deserve is to let go, which is far from a random act of courage. Dig deep down and summon your bravery.

Repel negative people however possible. There may be difficult conversations but the alternative is to continue to let others sap your energy and hold you back.

> **Repel negative people however possible.**

While you're at it, keep tabs on your own negativity. You may not realize how much you complain. How serious are the things that bother you? Put it into context. Are you complaining about a negative experience in a restaurant or is it about your doctor's misdiagnosis? Catch yourself and try to be objective about whether it is justified. Could it be that you are complaining for the sake of complaining?

Could this be a sign that you're someone who lets negativity build up inside you like a pressure cooker and your complaints are like a release valve? If this point resonates with you, then please consider how holding onto that energy is bad for your health as well as that of those closest to you.

If all you do is complain without trying to make things better, then the complaint is in the mirror. Minimize the negativity and save yourself and others from the stress. As the saying goes, "Don't sweat the small stuff."

> **Head off sources of stress by drawing on compassion and empathy. Patience is everything.**

Whenever possible, head off sources of stress by drawing on compassion and empathy. Patience is everything. Imagine yourself having limitless patience and compassion until you actually do. I understand that's a tall order.

Another worthy question to ask yourself with brutal honesty is who, if anyone, do you allow to judge you? Do you internalize those opinions and allow that energy to impact your well-being? Consider what it would be like to flat-out stop caring what others, or at least certain individuals, think of you. How freeing would that feel and what positive energy would you draw from trusting your own opinion?

If you find yourself at peace with all the members of your Tribe, that's phenomenal! Here's a good time for you to consider what you can do to enrich those relationships to create more fulfillment.

Increasing positivity and bringing more joy into life doesn't have to be difficult or strange. We all manage energy in one way, shape or form every day. It's not-so-simply a matter of applied will.

Here's an idea. Make a proactive choice to expand your Tribe. Go ahead. Choose 3 acquaintances in your periphery. It could be a work colleague, a friend of a friend or an acquaintance on social media. Now, go make friends. You're also free to invite more positive relationships and seek out more positivity from the ones you already have. Who in your life always makes you smile?

Let's get into action. Reach out and invite someone for coffee or an alternative beverage, unexpectedly. Chances are, at least if I were to lay odds, they'll have been just thinking about you. They'll almost surely be glad that you took the initiative to get together. Now, go have fun!

You'll also benefit from taking inventory of environmental influences that cause you to absorb negativity. A simple example is to take a "news diet." Let's face it, the news tends to be much more negative and it's all-too-easy to get sucked into the likes of anything from politics and world crises to disasters, pandemics and local tragedies.

That energy can take on a life of its own. The next thing you know, you find yourself in a heated exchange on social media that can sour or upend those relationships. Is it obvious that I am speaking from experience?

What environments and experiences feed your soul?

How can we not feel the effects of it all? In contrast, what environments and experiences feed your soul?

For some of us, there is also another matter of importance: our spiritual connection with a belief, trust and faith in G-d through one form of religion or another. That practice also has a lot to do with a sense of community. There are certain mystical and intangible aspects of whatever relationship we have with our spirituality.

Given that this is a very personal decision and a unique experience with many variables, we'll refrain from exploring this topic much further. I'm also pretty sure that being raised Jewish and attending a Catholic high school doesn't qualify me as a trained theologian or academic philosopher. We are not going to solve a many-a-millennia debate here.

We are not going to solve a many-a-millennia debate here.

It's fair to say that, among the many unsolvable things we experience in life, having faith is a reliable way to take comfort and make sense of the world around us. As such, one's faith also plays a significant role that filters and shapes our perceptions.

Having said all that about Managing Energy, we probably cannot close out without further exploring Karma. For those who believe in any aspect of it, you already know what Karma means to you. But, in however many ways anyone might believe in Karma, the common theme is one of energy transference, which is consistent with what we just covered.

Earlier we referenced the practicality of kindness. In the purest sense, the concept is oxymoronic. In and unto itself, true kindness isn't practical, it's about being selfless. However, in the realm of Karma, especially in the long run, kindness is entirely practical. For instance, if someone takes advantage of another, they may win in the short term. True Spiders get an emotional high out of it. Maybe they even make more of a profit. Aside from natural Karma, however that plays out, there are so many things that can go wrong, which are under the radar:

- That person can talk badly of them to someone else and they lose a business opportunity without even knowing about it.
- That person will never refer business to them, so they miss out on more opportunities.
- That person also may become very successful and more influential in the future.

Not being kind, such as by cheating others, simply doesn't make long-term business sense. One might benefit in the short term, but over 5 to 50 years, I doubt many people end up better for it. Kindness is not just good Karma, it stacks the odds in our favor in our careers and in life.

> *Instead of adapting to that energy in the room, try being the one to influence it.*

We'll encounter similar themes later when we touch on the well-established Law of Attraction and gratitude practices. Just remember that, when it comes to Karma, what comes around goes around. Spider-reminder: treat others as you would want others to treat you.

In closing, you will always encounter your share of cranky restaurant servers, among others, in social settings. Instead of adapting to that energy in the room, try being the one to influence it.

CHAPTER SEVEN

Being a Life Athlete

What we just covered about Managing Energy focuses on internal self-awareness about our own behaviors and interpersonal dynamics among others. Let's go back to the starting blocks and get into action with the fundamentals of human performance.

Here we'll find a combination of science and techniques about self-care that are worth sharing and supported by any number of experts, like Brendon Burchard.

Another book I'd like to recommend is *The Power of Full Engagement* by Jim Loehr and Tony Schwartz. It goes back a few years but provides sound approaches to maintaining a high quality of life.

As a premise, these guys started out by working with professional athletes and developed a system to help them perform at their best. Yet the tools they employed were not specific to their clients' sport or technical prowess. They were about what they view as the four pillars of how we align ourselves energetically.

Full Engagement takes the same system they used to help athletes at the very top of their game and applies it to the "business athlete." Though geared to help professionals, the foundation for personal development is universal. In my case, working for myself since 2002, my business and personal lives intertwine. That means this system applies beyond work to being a life athlete.

The authors focus on four separate, but related sources of personal energy and our ability to expend and recover each at their respective levels. They illustrate them as building one upon the other, much like Maslow's *Hierarchy of Needs*.

The foundation of this approach is about being *physically energized*. Its capacity is defined by the *quantity* of energy carried in our heart, lungs, abdominals, shoulders, back, legs and arms. Supportive habits and skills involve sleep, exercise, diet and hydration.

Being *emotionally connected* is the second tier, which is defined by the *quality* of energy found in our self-confidence, self-regulation, interpersonal effectiveness and ability to empathize. Supportive habits and skills involve patience, openness, trust and enjoyment.

Being *mentally focused* is the third tier. Its *capacity* is defined by the center of our energy as it also relates to realistic optimism, time management and creativity. Supportive habits and skills involve visualization, positive self-talk, a positive attitude and mental preparation.

Finally, the top level is for an individual to come into full energetic balance by being *spiritually aligned*, which they define by the *force* of our energy as it relates to character, passion/commitment, integrity and service to others. Supportive habits and skills involve honesty, integrity, courage and persistence. Note that this is not specific to religious faith as much as it is a broader belief system and strength of character.

Optimal performance requires the greatest quantity, highest quality, clearest focus and maximum force of energy. They explain how most of us are physically and spiritually under-trained (not enough stress) and mentally and emotionally over-trained (not enough recovery).

Develop positive rituals to bring it all together.

The book goes much deeper into these various facets of maximizing personal energy while including exercises to help you develop a practical approach to put these priorities into action. It provides strategies and practices to achieve optimal performance while teaching how to recognize and avoid the barriers to full engagement in the hopes that you develop positive rituals to bring it all together.

Given that you are someone interested enough in personal development to be reading this book, you are surely familiar with any number of "systems" to nurture progress. In fact, in studying the habits of high-performance individuals, Brendon Burchard isolates the "HP6" – Seeking Clarity, Generating Energy, Raising Necessity, Increasing Productivity, Developing Influence and Demonstrating Courage.

That said, the purpose here is to provide some favorable reviews of these books and explain how these authors have influenced me. These are *their* books. They have also worked hard to acquire earned expertise in their specialties. Check them out.

I believe it's also important to stay within my wheelhouse in sharing personal life experiences and perspectives. I encourage you to seek out other similar sources of information that resonate, motivate and guide you in related ways. The obvious reason for the consistency in emphasizing similar topics in various books is that they are tried and true.

One area in which I have gained a much deeper, first-hand appreciation is with nutrition. We all know the all-important adage of our body being a temple. It's also safe to say that many of us would have a lot more energy and be in better current and future health if we added healthier alternatives to our diets and consumed certain things in moderation.

However, in addition to Erica being the love of my life, she also happens to be a Certified Health Coach and advocate for an all-natural, organic diet. She went totally vegan and gluten-free this past year and it's done wonders for her. She also swears by the nutrition science behind Isagenix and has helped nearly 20,000 people to benefit from their offerings.

There seems to be a trend of how others tend to have a knee-jerk reaction about supplements. It still baffles me how people continue to be close-minded. I will be respectful and say very little here. We do owe the better parts of our health and freedom to Isagenix and its founding family. I am grateful and proud to express a moment of appreciation.

My personal mission to positively impact as many people as possible includes the importance of well-being. This is my *one and only* mention for anyone interested in learning about Isagenix to improve their health and fitness: our team site is IsaZinman.com. Either way, thank you for being cool with that!

Though I don't eat as healthily as my wife, I do appreciate weaving in the good stuff to help balance out my less-than-ideal consumption. It's apparent why physical health is the first tier of the energy management model. How we treat our bodies matters more than too many people ignore.

This all got me thinking about certain aspects of my lifestyle and belief system to maintain my overall well-being. Consistent with others, I view physical health activity as most essential. In my view, the other priorities are for sleep, nutrition and stress management.

Writing the book inspired me to develop what we'll call a Self-Care Report Card™ for you and others to track and rate yourselves, myself notwithstanding. Naturally, with 100 being the perfect score, the point system incorporates a weighted algorithm, again with physical activity being the highest point-getter followed by sleep and nutrition combined with hydration and managing stress levels on a weekly basis. The assessment for stress is scored in the opposite way as the other criteria, which is to say it's about how little stress was incurred, be it by having a peaceful number of days and, especially, your ability to prevent, mitigate and release the remaining, unavoidable occurrences.

Without further ado, for your viewing pleasure below, is your Self-Care Report Card broken down into these four vital needs and related health activities (downloadable at Z-isms.com). Again, the scoring system is meant to be very simple by referencing the optimal levels of activity for exercise, sleep, nutrition/hydration, and the all-too-easily overlooked factor of stress management.

Self-Care Report Card
Daily | Monthly | Weekly

Vital Need	Health Activity	Rating
Physical Activity	**Awesome:** *Either* 30 minutes of moderate-intensity cardio activity at least five days (150 minutes total) per week *or* at least 25 minutes of vigorous aerobic activity three days (75 minutes total) per week AND strength training for all muscle groups at least 2 times per week.[1] **Not Bad:** Anything between Awesome and Not Great. **Not Great:** Little to no exercise beyond routine daily life.	Awesome = 40 Not Bad = 30 Not Great = 10
Sleep Quality	**Awesome:** Between 7 to 9 hours per night at generally consistent times going to bed and awaking.[2] **Not Bad:** Between 6 to 7 hours per night and/or having an inconsistent schedule. **Not Great:** Under 6 hours per night (on average).	Awesome = 25 Not Bad = 15 Not Great = 10
Nutrition & Hydration	**Awesome:** For nutrition, you *know* how Awesome you've been or not. For hydration, consume the equivalent of eight 8-ounce glasses of water (for men) per day or 7 glasses (for women).[3] **Not Bad:** You know if you've been less than Awesome or Not Great. **Not Great:** Need we say more?	Awesome = 15 Not Bad = 10 Not Great = 5
Stress Management	**Awesome:** Stress is an unvoidable part of life. If you have had a stressful time, you proactively minimized or mitigated it and diminished that stress through exercise, meditation or some other coping skill.[4] **Not Bad:** Anything between Awesome and Not Great. **Not Great:** Your stress level causes obvious emotional or mental fatigue.	Awesome = 20 Not Bad = 10 Not Great = 0

GRADES: A = 85+   B = 70+   C = 55+   D = 40+   F = <40   **TOTAL:** ____

Guideline Sources:
1: U.S. Department of Health and Human Services
2: National Sleep Foundation
3: The Mayo Clinic (hydration)
   For nutrition: consult the Harvard Healthy Food Pyramid
4: National Institute of Mental Health

The baseline for the optimal activity levels for each category are sourced from the authorities for each criterion. The points and rating for meeting those benchmarks are designated as "Awesome." On the other hand, poor performance is scored as "Not Great," and everything in between as "Not Bad."

The Self-Care Report Card may not be perfect but I think you'll find it to be useful to benchmark and improve your healthy habits. Give it a try. Be more mindful of your daily activities so it's easy to grade yourself each week. Please feel free to let others know about the Report Card. Even if they don't read the book, they may still find it helpful as a self-accountability tool.

One final all-too-relevant point is that, if we cross-reference the Self-Care Report Card with the Mood Scale, we can incorporate mental and emotional health, especially for applying the 3-Day Rule to maintain that part of our well-being. Whether you're someone who has ever had to contend with mental imbalance or not, the essentials for taking the best care of yourself still apply.

In any case, I hope you put it to good use and that it adds a tool for minding the Mood Scale and taking better care of yourself. Maybe give it a try every day for a week and/or maybe once a week. See how it goes. You deserve it!

Before moving on from here, I believe it's essential to cover a point paid less attention to in the other books, and in life overall, which is about our individual self-esteem. It's at the very root of our ability to align our physical, emotional, mental and spiritual selves.

Though it's not the central purpose of Z-isms, this topic is surely at the foundation of multiple points in the book, especially about being the best life athlete. We have all heard the saying that we cannot love others until we love ourselves. There are quite a few books with this as their focus for personal development. However, please allow me to ask you to consider a certain way to approach this fundamental trait.

In short, it's to be the kind of person you wish you had in your life because you truly are all you've got. Instead of this being about treating others as you would wish them to treat you, it's to treat yourself in this way.

Nowhere on this planet is there someone just like you. You are the first you there has ever been or ever will be.

> *Nowhere on this planet is there someone just like you.*
>
> *You are the first you there has ever been or ever will be.*

But if you could meet your exact self as another person, would you like them? Would they be a good friend? Would they seem kind, genuine and loving? Would they have time and patience to invest in your friendship? Would you feel good in their presence? Would they make you laugh? Would you truly want to spend time with them? Would they be a good influence? Though it may seem a bit corny to say: no one spends more time with you than you.

Take a moment and be direct with yourself as you would with your best friend. How would you rate in the four areas among physical, mental, emotional and spiritual health? What have you done to achieve that rating? What might be some incremental improvements you could easily achieve and would build momentum?

If you catch yourself in the act of being unkind to yourself, as many of us often are, then consider what might be a loving approach. Do that instead, even if it doesn't feel natural at first. Practice unlearning self-abuse and just be kind to yourself. Just a friendly reminder: you deserve it. Really, you do.

Self-care is not an indulgence; it is a discipline. It requires pure determination, a deep and personal understanding of your priorities and a respect for both yourself and the people with whom you choose to spend your life. Be the kind of person you wish you had in your life. Though it may not apply to you, there are a significant number of people who have never forged a genuine relationship with themselves. If, for whatever wrong reason, you struggle to believe in yourself, start there.

> **Fulfillment and joy happen in the present moment.**

This brings us back to experiencing life in the now. Fulfillment and joy happen in the present moment. We live in an increasingly fast-paced world and the concept of slowing down and appreciating life even momentarily may seem like a waste of time. Accept the challenge to take one week to make a concerted effort to practice living in the present moment. Here's an exercise that could be a life-changer.

Though it's a little out there, what would it be like to have a whole Day of Silence? Start with no electronics! Just be with yourself. Try to notice all you can to the fullest extent, such as colors, shapes, textures, sounds, feelings, emotions, beauty or love. Spend time in nature and just be.

This probably seems more than a little odd and well beyond your comfort zone. That's the point. It's an exercise to help you integrate more joy into the rest of your daily life. That sounds worth it to me. Dare yourself to do it and experience the challenge.

> **Dare yourself to do it and experience the challenge.**

Along these lines, when you are with someone, be with them fully without thinking about what you will say or do next. Forget about tomorrow. Force yourself not to interrupt whoever has the floor. Be present. Listen to their words and the meaning behind them. Observe their body language. Tune in.

What else can you notice when you force yourself to remain present in the moment? Most of us are fortunate to be born with the ability to hear, among others. However, active listening is a learned skill that many people have never trained to develop. It *is* hard, but practice makes perfect.

Love what you do. Love talking to people. Ask them questions. Learn about them. Find ways to help them. Serve them. Fill a need. Share a resource.

We cannot achieve becoming a Life Athlete without embracing the most essential fuel to power your engine. Did you guess that I'm still referring to self-love as a basic human need?

> *Loving ourselves is foundational to living life.*

Loving ourselves is foundational to living life. When we experience self-love, we take better care of ourselves and make clearer decisions that propel us to be our best selves. Too many of us do not feel worthy of love and goodness and, therefore, gravitate towards self-sabotage.

We all have bad mornings or whole days. We get knocked down or off-balance. It's up to us to rebound, even if that means asking for help. Make a concerted effort to bolster your coping skills – be that by turning to exercise, your favorite music, funny videos, or a TV program. We covered some of this in perception and mood management. Whatever that is for you, keep your spirits up. Just in case you missed it, you deserve to be your best self and live your best life!

Most of us know that the more love we experience within and for ourselves, the more we attract it into our lives. As with many other core topics we're covering, this is like an unused muscle that needs conditioning. This comes down to forcing yourself to change behaviors and turn them into habits.

It may feel uncomfortable at first and involve a workout routine, but your self-esteem, enriched life and better self will thank you.

CHAPTER EIGHT

The Elements in Motion

Thinking back, it was nearly half a lifetime ago when a profound experience instilled me with a foundation for personal growth that I have relied on ever since.

It happened in Big Sur, California, at an unusual place called Esalen that operates like a commune. It's set on the Pacific cliffs where the highway winds along the water. This location easily comes to mind because it's where manufacturers of performance cars showcase them in commercials.

Aside from Esalen being a traditional commune, its claim to fame is that it's one of the few places on Earth where hot springs meet the ocean. There is a multimillion-dollar hot springs bathhouse built into the cliff above the Pacific. It's among the most beautiful places I've ever experienced.

My main purpose for being there was to visit a friend who worked as a grade school teacher for the kids living on the property. She kept pretty busy during the weekdays, so I decided to fill my time by taking an intensive workshop being offered that week.

The topic of the one I chose was the mind-body connection and movement.

The training was dense and intense. There were 3 instructors for only 7 participants. We discussed, acted out and practiced in many ways for about 36 hours over 6 days, along with doing some additional video work.

It was easy to tell I was the odd man out. My classmates joked about me being a "Philly Boy." They were right. At that age, I was kind of a stereotypical jock and wore my baseball cap backwards. I was definitely a foreigner among the Cali natives.

The part that made the workshop even more interesting is that it featured a model made up of the four elements: Earth, Air, Fire and Water. These were illustrated in a four-quadrant grid according to their natural motion. The training also got into how each element correlates with certain personality types and how they interact, especially situationally.

OK, all this seemed totally flaky at first. *Totally.*

It's a simple concept to comprehend that Fire plus Fire makes more Fire. Here we explored the various manners in which we would be confronted by Fire, such as by an angry person.

We addressed how to overcome our own natural aggressive reaction by grounding ourselves in that moment and making a conscious decision to behave like Water to douse the flames, even if and when that's not in ones' core nature.

In the case of a brewing argument, instead of letting ego get in your own way by focusing on being right about something, it becomes easier and better to diffuse a situation by making a conscious decision not to argue.

> **Two "rights" don't make a wrong.**

It's not about giving up the "I'm right" part as much as it is accepting that two "rights" don't make a wrong. There's also the variable of how different perceptions color the same circumstances. As discussed, two people can misunderstand or perceive the very same situation in completely opposite ways.

Staying carefully in control of aggressive impulses will empower you to overcome your ego and make a choice for the greater good. Motivated by the benefits of choosing not to argue, this is a core aspect of effectively Managing Energy.

After all, fighting Fire with Fire only spreads a blaze.

Here is where you might imagine sparing yourself hours of angry email threads or days of hashing out and retelling details (spreading Fire) to others you think are willing to listen. Such negativity requires reliving those events and emotions over and over and over again. All the while, you are unnecessarily imposing a destructive thought pattern and attitude upon yourself and among those closest to you.

Take the opportunity to be the bigger person. Having the forethought and composure to know that it's not worth wasting valuable energy makes it easier to empower yourself to opt for an alternative that will extinguish flames rather than add fuel. Yes, the other person may even be totally out-of-line but making yourself the priority is the key. Choose reconciliation over retaliation.

**Choose
reconciliation
over retaliation.**

How might behaving like Water play out in a moment like the following?

"Listen [person], I certainly see where you're coming from, but there's more than one way to view this situation. I just see it differently. You're absolutely entitled to your own opinion, just as I am. It's clear we don't agree about this and would be best to just leave it at that. I surely respect your position. There just doesn't seem to be any benefit to going on any further about it."

In short, *"I understand and respect your point. I have a different perspective. Let's leave it at that."* Even shorter is the option to say, *"There's no need to debate that point."*

What are they going to do? You've hand-cuffed them with kindness and stood your ground at the same time. Come to think of it, the response above might be more of an Earth-like approach of smothering a Fire with dirt. How did that feel? Aren't you glad you kept your cool? Nice going!

**I accept
full responsibility
for what happened.**

Here's another one: "I accept full responsibility for what happened." This works especially well in personal relationships. If something isn't worth a fight, just save yourself by taking the blame even if you know the other person is at some fault. This is the same point as someone saying, "pick your battles."

This is a good time to revisit that favorite anecdote: The best way to handle a crisis is to prevent it. If a heated argument can turn into something of an "Energy Cancer," then prevention is the cure. My apologies if that felt too harsh, but it's too true.

Today, some of the more common schools of thought for this involve emotional intelligence and conflict resolution. Exercising maturity is a good thing. These points also intersect with Earned Confidence, Managing Energy and combating Spiders.

There's much more worth sharing about how the four elements interact and this enlightening learning experience.

> *Make a conscious choice to stop an unnecessary argument.*

In this case, just remember to make the practical choice to come to your senses. You will take more pride in maintaining your composure and making a conscious choice to stop an unnecessary argument instead of getting hung-up on winning it. Just remain calm, plant your feet and reach for the fire extinguisher!

The next part of the experience had to do with how each element is most dominant within each of us. Thinking about it, if someone has a Type A personality, they almost surely personify Fire.

Now that you are familiar with Fire and its combustibility, let's look at the full model with the other elements.

As described, the four natural elements are positioned and illustrated in respective quadrants. Based on a framework of the mind-body connection, it factors the directional movements and positions of each element as well as associates their distinct personality traits.

Stay with me.

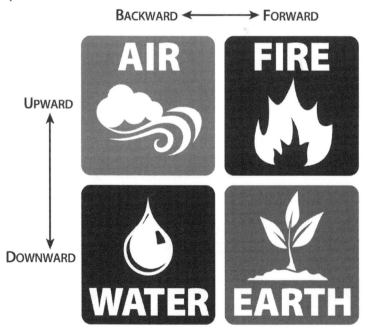

Z-isms: Insights to Live By

Viewing the diagram, you see that Water and Earth are positioned in the bottom quadrants just the same as they exist on the ground in nature. The other elements are also consistent with Air being upward as it is in the sky. Fire, which takes a gaseous form by consuming all in its path, has a forward and upward trajectory.

What else did we do for those 36 hours over six days? It was multifaceted. Part of it was discussing the elements in motion and acting each out. In pretending to be Air, we swirled off one another. If we were Water, we repelled one other backward with equal force. This was definitely the weirdest part of the course, but I went with it.

> *The various ways we explored how the elements interact were multidimensional.*

Though the quadrant grid is illustrated as a two-dimensional image, the various ways we explored how the elements interact were multidimensional.

The one aspect that has stuck with me the most over the years is how each of the elements relate to various personas. Again, it's easy to determine that most everyone with a Type A personality belongs in the Fire quadrant. These individuals often walk more purposefully and appear to tilt forward when in motion.

The next time you have a layover, look around the airport and notice how people walk. Even if there are some non-Type A individuals trying to make their flight, you're still likely to pick them out of the crowd.

With Air, think of someone who is more laid back. Things seem to just roll off their shoulders. They are flighty and aloof. Being upward and in the backward position in relation to Fire, Air characterizes those more typically viewed as a Type B personality. The stereotypical "surfer dude" would be Air-dominant.

If there was a conventional version of describing someone as Type C, it would be Water, which embodies the most passive personality. Their motion can be illustrated by thinking of a canoe.

What happens when you give it a push? Naturally, it floats away from you without resistance and in equal force to that push.

As with Air in the backward quadrant, they are non-confrontational. These individuals fit into the same category as those we might think of as a pushover or marshmallow. However, for Air, that is more of a conscious decision whereas, for those more Water-dominant, it's more of an innate, involuntary response. Unfortunately, it may also be symptomatic of conditioning among victims of abuse.

The dynamics in the forward-facing quadrants are similar. Fire is more prone to fly off the handle, while Earth-dominant individuals are more like conscientious objectors. Yet when applied as illustrated, Water can be very powerful when it comes to taming and extinguishing Fire, among all else.

Additional aspects of the remaining element, Earth, are straight-forward, and I mean that literally. Someone Earthy is grounded as if they are deeply and strongly rooted. They are the neutral element who will neither push nor can they be pushed. They stand their ground.

It's very cool how they all fit together. I've encountered numerous models to distinguish personalities, most typically as they relate to fostering teamwork and mitigating conflict in professional settings. Larger companies often invest tens of thousands of dollars to label people different colors, determine the likes of every employee's "spirit animal," or whatever. You get the idea.

> **This model has stood the test of time.**

But, at least for me, in representing the interactive movements among the natural elements, this model has stood the test of time.

Getting back to our originally scheduled topic about the workshop, we delved even deeper to determine how each of us possesses an innate element with which we are born. It may be an overreach to say it's the one that fits our childhood temperament.

We then further explored how each of us also has a secondary element to which we gravitate and is used mainly in taming ourselves. Could one's ability to change their dominant element be a result of maturation? Does that lend itself to revisiting the notion of "Nature vs. Nurture" we considered about Spiders vs. non-Spiders? What do you think?

Have you identified your core element yet?

Have you identified your core element yet? This would be based on the tendencies of your behavior and responses to external stimuli. You may have already self-assessed the element you innately personify as well as whether your life experiences, with wisdom and maturity, have changed the element with which you currently identify.

When faced with a situation that prompts a "Fight or Flight Response," your prime element is almost surely Fire if you're prone to fight, though it may be Earth if you're just not one to back down. If you are more likely to take flight or retreat, you're almost surely predisposed to be Water or Air.

In examining the elements for myself, it's easy to recognize that Fire is my natural default but my disposition in day-to-day life is Earth-dominant. While I'm driven by a certain passion and intensity, my wife and kids will attest that I have a reservoir of patience and can be maddeningly even-keeled. Of course, we all have our thresholds.

This model is very primal when we get right down to it. I think you'll find its simplicity resonates and that it adds something useful to your mindfulness toolbox. There's where you should already find your newly heightened Spider Senses, Earned Confidence, prevention tactics, perception perspectives, mood monitoring and healthy ways for Managing Energy.

Even so, it's not as though you'll go around pointing at everyone in your life on a daily basis while labeling them as Fire with an Earthy maturity or Water with a little bit of Earth and Air character traits. Then again, you might. I did at first.

How about taking this one for a spin like we did with our Spider Senses Exercise? Think of 5 to 10 family members, friends, coworkers or other people in your life. Are they Fire, Air, Earth, or Water? You shouldn't have to overthink it. You'll likely find it more of a simple and fun exercise than something to do all the time with everyone you meet. Feel free to go with that.

> *You shouldn't have to overthink it.*

For me, now nearly 20 years later, it's really something I turn to more when I encounter life circumstances that warrant self-reflection or conflict resolution. This might be when I find myself weakening and stressing or swimming against the current and squaring off with a vicious Spider.

Darn you, Aunt Jane!

There's one last memory I would like to share about something that happened during this experience. The workshop was held in a house-like building among many others across the Esalen property. The house on the campus where our class was held was positioned on stilts that actually extended it halfway over the edge of the ocean cliff.

Now that you have a sense of this experience, it should come as no surprise that part of what we did was practice meditation. There I was sitting on the floor of the far side of the house with eyes closed, knees crossed and wearing my baseball cap backward in true fashion.

One thing I definitely recall being a distraction during that meditation was how much I disliked sitting with my knees crossed. They just don't quite go that way. Not much has changed. I need to stretch more! That's probably about when I was instructed to refocus on my breathing and to quiet my mind.

> *My impatience was*
> *immediate as*
> *I continued to feel*
> *like it wouldn't stop.*

Anyway, at that moment all those years ago, I suddenly had a nauseating sensation and could feel vibrations and jolting. It only lasted a few seconds but felt much longer. My impatience was immediate as I continued to feel like it wouldn't stop. Not realizing in that very moment, it was a bona fide California earthquake!

Had a more powerful quake and its epicenter been closer to Big Sur, those stilts could have collapsed right there and then and the Pacific would have swallowed me whole. Okay, a gratuitous over-dramatic point made. It's not as though the incident qualified for my shortlist of near-death experiences, just in case you're wondering.

It's been a lot of fun to share this experience with you as something that continues to resonate for me after all this time. I hope you find it provides some *Insights to Live By*, at least when it comes to understanding and interacting with others as well as within yourself. Here's the best nature photo I've ever taken.

CHAPTER NINE

Swim with the Current

Just about everyone knows the expression, "Go with the flow." It's an integral part of what we've covered about energy, movement and the topics that lie ahead.

Being in the flow is a personal experience. Can you think of everyday examples of feeling the current? Well, an easy one is experiencing a "hot streak" while in a gambling establishment. Some people call it luck. If you're someone who believes in luck, on what are you basing that conclusion?

Seriously, take a minute to think it through. Do you refer to it as "blind luck?" That doesn't sound too certain. Whichever way the chips may fall, with any luck you'll know when to cash in and still have something lining your pockets.

How about that feeling when you make every traffic light while in route from one place to another? Okay, we probably need to yield to the naysayers who may counter that example as a function of sensible municipal planning. Fair enough.

What about experiencing the flow in ways that begin to border on coincidence? How about getting the perfect parking space in an overcrowded lot at the very moment you needed or expected it? The same goes for that choice table at a busy restaurant or scoring amazing seats to a concert or sporting event.

How does it feel when you're "in the zone?"

We seem to be getting closer to articulating the experience, but the most accurate examples are among those that each of us find meaningful.

What feels unusual to you? How does it feel when you're "in the zone?"

A tangible one for me is playing cards with Jake. More specifically, we have our thing of playing Uno in restaurants, which we've done since he was three. I've no doubt we've played tens of thousands of hands in the now 15+ years we've been at it.

We don't experience the flow every time we play. It's more like every 5 to 10 times that there are long stretches that are too apparent to be random. It's happened so many times that we were able to notice some patterns in how the cards flow.

Poor winners make sore losers.

This often occurs when the other person acts overly confident. That's when the momentum shifts and they might lose 10+ hands in a row. Or, suddenly, there are 3 or 4 in a row that have massive points. We even have an expression:

"He who talks trash often eats it."

Put another way: Poor winners make sore losers.

Like I said, this has been our experience. It may not be what others observe.

Hopefully, you encounter a healthy share of positive, flow-like experiences that you find meaningful and bring you joy. It can be difficult to sustain being in the flow given all the curveballs life throws us. As we'll soon discuss, the key to connecting and reconnecting to that feeling is to proactively weave gratitude into your daily life.

Of course, it's also about mindfulness and picking up on cues. When we see that something is trending through external events or internal observations, that may be a good opportunity to assess which way the current flows.

Let's change directions. Naturally, one way to discuss this refers to when our Water element is faced with Fire. There are certain times when the flow of any given interaction leads one to take a pause, be that to douse flames or choose to be entirely non-confrontational.

A common indicator of swimming in the wrong direction is when you feel like you've been "banging your head against the wall" for whatever reason. In general, if you experience a certain level of stress and you are not entirely sure why, that's when you need to check in with yourself. This is your alarm system. The same applies to when you find yourself in the "try and try again" mode. By the time you get to the third try, it may be time to alter the definition of what success means to you.

When we talk about how things flow, however, it's more than just an expression. There is something more palpable to it, be that the influence of energy woven into life circumstances, someone infecting others with their bad mood, or a Spider up to no good. Something is just wrong. You don't have to know exactly what it is.

Trust your gut! It's time to ask what and/or *who* is the current?

> **It's time to ask what and/or who is the current?**

Here's where you confront the situation and ask, "What are my options to go in another direction for what I'm trying to accomplish?" Then ask, "Which among those options would most feel like enough of an opposite direction that I would be swimming with the current instead of against it?"

More often, doing this applies to more significant life decisions. It may be about mounting frustrations at a dead-end job or constant stress with a coworker, particularly a supervisor or another superior. What else might you do if you were to leave that job, free yourself of that stress and make happiness your priority? Maybe it's time to pursue that business you have always wanted to start. Work the numbers!

We can't slight the necessity to provide for oneself and one's family. More and more employers subscribe to the benefits of rotational job mobility where employees can change departments or take an entirely different position within the company. Maybe it's time to explore that possibility.

What might you do to change the frequency with that irritating coworker that would bring needed relief? You might rely on tools like the interaction of elements and decide that it's better to stop behaving as Fire and douse the flames with Water. Or, you can make a conscious choice to be Airy and just let it roll off your shoulders.

Reflecting on Managing Energy, there's the prime example about severing or insulating a personal relationship. It might be your significant other or someone who needs to be a former member of your Tribe. Be honest with yourself. If you can only see that relationship as a dead end, or you have lost hope in someone unwilling to change, it's time to put yourself first. What does that mean to you?

It's time to put yourself first.

Leaving a secure but dysfunctional job or relationship is hard. Summon your Earned Confidence with eyes wide open. You've got this! It's also essential to seek balance and take stock of your most important life priorities where you *are* swimming with the current.

Instead of some external example, here's where it helps to get a bit more personal.

My wife and I have never quite had what I would call a full-on fight, which is even more significant because both of us are willful individuals. Of course we disagree at times. Rarely would I ever say we have disagreed in any major way. We've also only been together for 3 years at this point, so I have no misgivings that it won't happen. But, here and now, what makes me certain to assert this personal fact is that this is not the first go-around for either of us. I have been in a marriage where fighting became too much of the norm. I know what a fight is.

> *Am I about to disclose the true secret to a healthy marriage?*

Getting to the point, there's a very specific reason why our marriage is harmonious. Am I about to disclose the true secret to a healthy marriage, one of life's greatest mysteries? Well, with practice, you can decide for yourself.

For us, the key to marital harmony is that we always know where and *who* is the current at any given time. This applies to everything from who is better at what to any topic of discussion that requires one decision or the other. Of course, having the benefit of experience from our past relationships plays a significant role.

Knowing who is better at what is easy to discern, at least for us. Only one of us can be the foreman. Someone must lead and someone must yield. Better yet, one of us has to be the First Mate. There are also times that we enjoy tackling tasks together, like when she's Head Chef and I'm Sous-Chef.

> *It's the domestic version of going with the flow.*

Think about it. Go down the list with your significant other on who's better at what in everyday life and who does what around the house or otherwise. There's a comfort to having answers that make the doing easy and second nature. In other words, it's the domestic version of going with the flow.

It's a straight-up compatibility test. Some examples include: home repairs, shopping, controlling the TV remote, trash and recycling duties, doing laundry, pet care or landscaping. I do the driving and Erica enjoys being driven. By the way, I do my own laundry.

Of course, the current flows both ways. I'm very happy to have her play to her strengths, such as managing our house design and repair, the finances and her amazing gardening skills that make our home beautiful. Erica was also a counterintelligence agent for the U.S. Army, so it almost goes without saying that I find it just as easy to see things her way.

We decide together who leads and who yields.

Only one person can wear the pants at a time. Like I said, we almost always know which way the current flows. On the rare occasion that we don't see things the same way, we decide together who leads and who yields.

One loose end regards whatever both of us mind doing, which is a good time to rely on service providers, when possible. The other aspect to not overlook is if there are any "hot spots." A big one for us is who makes support calls. Erica loses patience and cracks the stress meter in no time flat, whereas I really don't mind handling those calls.

To me it's a simple matter-of-fact situation to get to a necessary result. I do not see the point in losing patience or taking that frustration out on someone who is just doing their job, even if they're not perfect at it.

In fact, I recently had a complex support call that took more than 3 hours. It wasn't easy, but it wasn't too hard either. More importantly, I was able to have the energy to jump to my next task instead of out the window.

Sure there are times when we softly butt heads. That triggers an alert to bring a discussion into better focus. The real question comes back to that conscious decision about asserting one's will as being the current. To whom does something matter more? Who has the most to lose or gain based on who handles what? There's also something to be said for being the one to yield. In most cases, that's an easy decision, especially if its one less thing to do.

If you are in a certain relationship or friendship involving some sort of friction or a simple sticking point, consider the strength and direction of that current and decide together about the point of least resistance.

In another example of flow and energy, every once in a while, though rare, I will meet someone who I severely dislike for whatever inexplicable reason. This can even happen without one word. Call it Spider Senses or my inner-Fire igniting.

> **Sometimes the best way to go with the flow is to not step in the current.**

There's a palpable repulsion, like how two magnets of the same polarity cannot be joined. My primal instinct to meeting someone I dislike is to repel them, keep my shields up, and pretty much never interact with them again or at all. Sometimes the best way to go with the flow is to not step in the current.

In a similar fashion, every so often, something happens, or there's a circumstance that strikes a chord within me that pretty much turns me into a dog with a bone. My response in dealing with a situation that causes lockjaw is to not let go until I see it through. Put another way, this is about making oneself the current with the strength of willpower and pushing forward in an assertive manner.

As rarely as this occurs, there's a fresh example worth sharing on many levels. In this case, a certain service provider had locked us into a strict contract. Time and time again, we have had nothing but negative experiences with the company. What bothers me most is how they conduct business and the obvious negative energy among their employees. As extreme as it may sound, this company is akin to an Evil Empire. Can you relate?

Then something happened recently that was the proverbial last straw. It's one of those things that caused me to decide that this company is not getting another dime from us. It's a matter of principle. Then, it was go-time!

> *It's a matter of principle. Then, it was go-time!*

I let Erica know that she needed to call the credit card company to stop a payment. This is where the plot thickens because my decision drew my wife into the situation with me. She was the one who chose this provider and signed the contract, so she's the one who must call her bank to block the automatic withdrawals. Her initial reaction was less than favorable, especially since I made a unilateral decision to cancel this service.

For me, having to ask this of her adds even more frustration. Dealing with this kind of situation lies squarely in my department. Now I have no choice but to cause my wife some stress. Worse yet, I first communicated this situation to her via text.

Nobody's perfect and I was far from it in that moment.

This isn't only my department, it's also about the farthest thing from Erica's. She would rather have a root canal. She also had some legitimate concerns, especially given that our being locked into this contract presents the potential consequence of hurting her credit. I believe you can relate. Like I said, Evil Empire!

Realizing her concerns were legit, I basically conveyed two things to my wife. One, when I say that someone is not getting another dime from us, she knows that I am the current. However, knowing she has a valid concern, I reassured her that, "Whatever happens here, however this goes down, I will make sure the outcome will have no negative impact on us and your credit. And, I will take it from here."

There's probably a simpler way to say that but this was no simple matter. She didn't need to take a hint. Her mind was put at as much ease as possible and there was no need or point about getting into anything more about it. That was a close one!

At this point, I've got the ball. Whatever remaining hassle was involved, Erica was insulated. It was time to apply some willpower. This being one of my strengths, I honestly don't want to seem like a braggart. All I'll say is that this is when I'm a man on a mission.

> *Stoking one's own Fire can be advantageous, provided we don't burn ourselves.*

This is to illustrate a very conscious choice to be the current. This is also a case when stoking one's own Fire can be advantageous, provided we don't burn ourselves by going too far.

The remaining details of this story are less relevant. In case you're curious, the short of it is that, in addition to the stopped payment, I called the credit card company to get the prior month's charge refunded and to have them on our side. The rest was just some back and forth with the local provider and their corporate office.

It took some doing but I held my ground. I explained this to be a matter of principle that prevents them from getting another dime. If they choose not to agree to zero-out our balance and threaten our credit, I would make my case on social media, add my thoughts to their online reviews and basically inform everyone I know what I think of their company.

I am pleased to report that the matter is fully resolved.

Going with the flow isn't exclusive to major events or encounters. In fact, in terms of the quality of everyday life, it's a simple matter of adaptability. The key here is to become hyper self-aware when you experience frustration, especially about something unexpected.

Case in point, I literally just stopped by the store to pick something up only to discover that my order was wrong. Correcting it would take about 10 to 15 minutes. I could have sat there and stewed about having to wait and being delayed from getting to my next destination. Instead I made good use of that unexpected time by picking up a few other supplies that were running low. I occupied my time while saving myself from having to get those supplies next week. It felt good to adapt.

The other loose end was the clerk. I knew he felt bad about the mistake and, upon finishing my order, he apologized profusely. I made a conscious effort to put him at ease that it wasn't his error and not to worry. It gave me the opportunity to get some other things done. I then was mindful to thank him by making eye contact and just taking the extra moment to let him know I was happy with their service and to have a great day. To put it another way, even for any given 10 minutes of your life, whenever the current shifts, swim in that direction.

> **Whenever the current shifts, swim in that direction.**

Let's move on and swim a few strokes in some of life's stronger currents beyond routine reactions, decisions about discontinuing a service provider and fighting an evil contract. Now we're in the waters of being in a bad marriage or feeling trapped in a job. It's harder to catch one's breath while being weighed down by even greater stress that compromises well-being and ones' livelihood. There's that stress theme repeating again. Once more, if possible, turn around no matter what the cost.

Before we wind down, I think it's important to revisit the topic of marriage and relationships. The whole point about knowing which spouse is the current also applies to Gladwell's "thin slicing" in *Blink*. You will recall the book's core focus was about proving how those who trust their gut with decisions make at least as good, if not better decisions as those who overthink data points in the proverbial analysis paralysis. This concept of thin-slicing refers to identifying singular data points that represent all we would need to know about something in order to base a decision.

The example to which Gladwell referred in the book that still sticks with me had to do with a study someone did on what makes marriages succeed or fail. The study revealed that a marriage or relationship is essentially unfixable once there is 'contempt' for one another.

It might be time to confront yourself, the situation and your significant other. What does your gut tell you about who is the current and your best course of action? Don't get me wrong, divorce is flat-out awful. There is no other way but through that hardship. A key question to consider is what one sets their sights on beyond that relationship and, if any kids are in the equation, how the family dynamic will change on the other side.

Divorcing my first wife was one of the toughest decisions in my life. Jake was only 2. Think man and baby alone in an apartment sterilizing bottles, changing diapers and reading and singing him to sleep. It was a sacrifice that I wouldn't change for the world, which is why having him half the time mattered everything to me.

What weighed on me most heavily in making that gut-wrenching decision is knowing it's more important that my son not grow up in a home full of stress and that I could be my best self for him as a father. The higher priority was for him to have balance. Now that he is starting his college days, it's an understatement to know that decision is among my best ones and how being a single dad has shaped us both for the better, including now with our having Erica and Greta in our lives.

I share this part of my private life because of how essential it is for you to confront this very question. It starts with challenging yourself. How can I be happier living the life I do? Is my relationship or marriage beyond contempt and the joy in it unrecoverable?

If you are experiencing true, incessant, toxic contempt in a relationship that seems as if it's already over, turn around before you drown.

> ***If it's already over, turn around before you drown.***

More to the point is that you as well as your significant other have one life to live and both may be better off letting go of one another. There's no way around it or to make it easier. Being the one to initiate leaving someone is one of life's scariest and most difficult decisions. It's also why too many people suffer instead. They are unable to summon the courage to move on. That said, the main point I'm trying to reinforce is that whenever you experience that feeling of swimming upstream, find your flow and swim with the current!

This topic is paramount. I cannot overstate how this reference to the flow of life has a certain palpable energy, often more than others. The main reason for emphasizing this relates to Managing Energy and how the flow and experience of "being in the zone" are a constant. This differs from various topics in other chapters that may be more situational and circumstantial.

The current is always there but may only be more palpable when it strengthens in either direction. Some people are never conscious of it. Others may only experience it in random flashes. Those who practice mindfulness have their own interpretations. At the very least, I believe it offers another data point to consider when making important decisions. Ultimately, the degree to which that's true is a factor of self-trust.

Just to reiterate one last time, when it truly feels like your arms are getting tired or your head hurts from banging it against a wall about something or someone, take a pause. Recalibrate your compass and change course towards wherever you find the current flows.

Wishing you safe, happy and fulfilling travels!

CHAPTER TEN

Making
Coincidences Matter

Now that we have a sense of being in the flow of life's current, the next sensible question to consider is about when we experience something more. For instance, what's the deal with coincidences and how can we make them matter?

But first, let's confirm that we know how to navigate this mystifying topic by checking in with Mr. Webster so we're certain our exploration is on course.

Coincidence
(Noun) co-in-ci-dence [koh-in-si-d*uh*ns]

> *A striking occurrence of two or more*
> *events at one time apparently by mere chance,*
> *often by time or place but seem*
> *to have some connection.*

It sounds like a reliable point of origin. However, since at least one type of coincidence is unique to individual experiences and elated perceptions, the true meaning may be within each one of us. Might we view coincidences any differently or expound on that supposed official definition?

> **What makes chance "mere?" Is that what you believe?**

The part I find most striking is where it says, "apparently by mere chance." Apparently to whom? What makes chance "mere?" Is that what you believe?

At what point does an occurrence or singular experience crossover from something random to something more? We can chalk it up to perception to a degree. It's more than that, right?

It's actually more like the opposite. There are facts and factors involved. Have you ever noticed how many of what you might describe as true coincidences are borne out of conversations with others you barely know? You will often notice it when the topic of discussion takes an unexpected turn. Therefore, you only discovered the coincidence because of the tangent that had no reason for coming up.

Maybe that's just me. Do your observations reflect a similar pattern? Think about it.

I wonder about that myself. Yet, no matter how we question it, the phenomenon really comes back to what each of us experience, perceive and process. There's no science here. These are mere observations over time. In fairness, if interested, there is a fair amount of science that's been conducted by mathematicians, statisticians and data analysis experts. It's easy enough to find and anything but easy to understand.

> **I believe that coincidences are indicators of being in the flow.**

Personally, I believe that coincidences are indicators of being in the flow. The energy is more often imperceptible or goes unnoticed but, like gravity, is always there.

It's natural to ponder why coincidences happen. Maybe it means

I need to follow through about something. I have found the best kind of coincidence involves some follow up action that leads to a more meaningful experience, connection with someone or creates a B-line to achieve something.

Or, for any cynics out there, maybe the only reason that happens is a result of my trying to assign meaning to the coincidence and it's my efforts in that aftermath being the true reason for those outcomes. Then, once I make those happen, it validates something unrelated in the first place. Personally, I've found that the negative predisposition of cynics is more skewed and makes them less credible.

A lighter, more mainstream version of coincidences is when we experience something a minimum of three times. Have you ever heard that one? When some sort of event, person, topic and the like comes up for you, especially in rapid succession, there is nothing wrong with exploring why.

There's everything right about having more fun!

If you fear what others may think of you, then keep it to yourself. Then again, tell the world if you prefer. There's everything right about having more fun!

Now let's go big and consider the coincidences that might fall into the category of being mathematically astronomical. These beg the question, "What are the odds?" It's these seemingly impossible events that make us take coincidences more seriously.

In fact, a key point of reference is that the more I pay attention and experience being in the flow, the more frequently I encounter coincidences. As a result, they also tend to become increasingly unusual and momentous. There are plenty of themes intersecting here. Let's ground ourselves with a few examples.

One of the more significant coincidences I experienced was about 15 years ago with a guy named Bruce. I had only a vague awareness of him until I walked into the local Harley-Davidson dealership.

There was Bruce, standing behind a kiosk where he set up shop to sell insurance to motorcycle enthusiasts.

The conversation began routinely enough and, then, led to the "you look familiar" comment. How cliché. We began trying to figure out how we knew one another. We uncovered that he's in the local Mason's lodge with my brother, David. "Yeah, I'm that Zinman," I said. My brother and Bruce knew one another, but that didn't explain why we thought we had met before.

Then, inexplicably, we get to where we grew up. My parents built a house in the Philly burbs just before I arrived on the scene. The area is called Huntingdon Valley. "I lived in HV, too," Bruce said, asking me to describe where.

It was a section called Albidale.

"Really? That's where I lived. What street were you on?" he asked.

"Bobwhite Lane," I said.

He lit up. "No flipping way! I lived on Bobwhite Lane, too! Which house were you?"

"733 Bobwhite," I responded.

Long story short, Bruce had also lived at 733 Bobwhite Lane in the very same house my parents built. We were able to go room by room and describe every detail from the fireplace in the split-level family room right down to the ugly green and white metal-crossed fence still there after all these years. It was very cool and a bit eerie at the same time. He had lived there with his girlfriend for several years who happened to have bought the house from the family who purchased it from my parents.

It almost seems as though this coincidence is downright unbelievable, yet it happened. Does that sound like mere chance to you? More to the point, what did it mean?

Aside from my getting my bike insurance through Bruce and having a conversation about my brother, all I can point to as of this day is that I am still in touch with him. If only there was a grander finale to explain why this coincidence mattered.

Given that I still know Bruce, maybe something more significant lies ahead. However, it is consistent with the fact that I had no business getting into that conversation with an insurance salesman in a motorcycle shop. For what it's worth, I am pretty sure we'd never met.

A more recent coincidence happened just last year, which was more business-related than it was personal. I'll try to keep this story tight but it involves some fine details. This coincidence occurred as part of my day job with The Internship Institute. The intersection of this happenstance involved a prior, routine email introduction to a guy named Greg who runs a start-up company with a bright future. Then there's Larry, a business partner prospect with a minor league professional team. This also intersects with another project at the time to help disadvantaged youth gain work experience to build the skills to make them more employable.

Larry and I had plans for lunch. I met him at their new stadium, got the grand tour and we went to the local Waterfront where there are various restaurants. It was a busy Friday and we ended up choosing a popular place.

Upon arrival, we were told there was a 45-minute wait. However, there was the option to sit at the bar upstairs, which made sense. We walked up there only to find every seat taken. However, there were two places at the corner of the bar where bar stools could be. So we did what strapping thirsty men do when they need bar stools, we grabbed a couple and made way to claim our perfect seats.

It's relevant to mention that I was on the inside stool with Larry to my left and that there were two guys to my right. As we settled in, Larry and the one closest to me recognized one another. Larry had been one of the guy's first customers and the guy explained how he, just then, had 17 employees and so forth. As I half-listened, I heard the guy say something that sounded a lot like the company to which I was introduced via email just the day before.

That's right, as it happens, this guy wasn't any of the other 16 employees at his company. It was Greg, the guy to whom I was introduced separately. Had Larry not been one of Greg's first customers, I would just as well have sat next to Greg for the next hour and never been the wiser that we'd just gotten acquainted by email.

Some time has passed since, and the opportunities to work together are still progressing. If nothing else, it's a fun ice-breaker with them both. I'm still in touch with Larry and other things are taking shape. For one, he's President of the Delaware Blue Coats, an American professional basketball team of the NBA G League and is an affiliate of my hometown Philadelphia 76ers.

With Greg, that coincidence mattered at the very least by helping us hit it off, though the outcome to cultivate opportunities for disadvantaged kids isn't too hard of a sell.

Lastly, here's a quick one from some years back when I was pushing a cart around one of those massive club stores. I turned the corner of some remote aisle and there was my oldest brother, Mark. It was a relatively basic coincidence until, not even a minute later, Dave showed up.

None of us knew the others were there and we hadn't seen one another in some time. We also could have been in that huge store at the same time and never have run into one another. Instead, we converged. So we made this coincidence matter by taking the opportunity to make dinner plans. We had a great time.

> *We could easily fill multiple books about astonishing coincidences.*

We could easily fill multiple books with stories about astonishing coincidences. I originally included more examples, but it was too much. These served their purpose. I can only speak for myself on this topic and am limited to a certain extent because these experiences are unique to each of us. However, my sense is that I encounter more coincidences than most others and that the odds of those that occur are more unusual.

What makes this spectrum of coincidences occur for some people more than others? Surely part of it is that I pay attention. For me, these and many other examples indicate that it's more than that. It's analogous to the discernable patterns I shared about swimming with the current. Ultimately, it's up to us to observe and decide for ourselves.

As mentioned, whether there's anything to it or not, I also believe that it's important to contemplate what it means to follow through on the coincidences that I encounter. It's more like trying to solve something by taking the hint to experience a life adventure. All of that could lead to something meaningful that is beyond ourselves. It may be as simple as it being the impetus for a conversation and the icebreaker that helps forge the bond of a valued friendship. Most often, I've found coincidences to be opportunities.

> *I've found coincidences to be opportunities.*

This topic is also beginning to border on that of Karma, which we touched upon with Managing Energy. It's still extremely tempting to dive into a bunch of other coincidences and you can probably tell that I'm more enamored about them than most people. What can I say? They're cool!

One final dimension about coincidences is the extent to which they occur independently from ourselves versus our role and, beyond that, our ability to cause them. If some people experience more and odder coincidences than others, it stands to reason that we are, at the very least, some part of the equation. Could the differential be a simple factor of varying degrees of mindfulness?

To what extent might coincidences be examples of Managing Energy and being in a synchronous flow with others regarding how we encounter the world around us? The simplest form of this often occurs among those with whom we share a certain connection. We might text or email one another at the exact same time. It may be when one person was just thinking of someone, maybe for the first time in quite a while, and then you hear from them that day. What is that?

Do you think there is any truth to incidences among twins that border on extrasensory perception? The evidence is anecdotal at best. We're just having some fun with this. However, I do believe that these seemingly inexplicable types of coincidences are energy exchanges indicative of the interconnectedness among sentient beings. That's us.

If the scientific notion about human beings only using 10 percent of our brains is accurate, what could we do with the other 90 percent? Maybe humankind will learn the answer one day. For now, I trust that this has something to do with intuition.

> *It's that thing between instinct and reason.*

More specifically, intuition involves one's ability to know something directly without conscious, analytical reasoning. It's that thing between instinct and reason. It has something to do with accessing unconscious knowledge, cognition and pattern recognition. It's getting easier to feel a bit lost as this topic gets more complex.

Here's another story to drive home the point. Some years back, I had a project for my marketing company involving a client in the telecommunications industry. They wanted to better understand the customers that call their service and why. Thing is, conventional market research methods would be ineffective. The audience here is very specific and very private, which is to say that even if we found a representative sample, the results would be skewed because these individuals would be less forthcoming.

Why? Because the unusual service this client provided was a psychic hotline. If your pessimism meter just spiked, stay with me. The clients who call the hotline see it as a guilty pleasure either for entertainment purposes or are motivated by sincere personal belief.

Knowing that asking probing questions of customers would be unreliable, the only method that seemed logical to gather accurate data was for me to speak with the psychics themselves. The client agreed. These individuals more commonly regard themselves as "Intuitives" with a combination of giftedness and clairvoyance. Certainly, if there was any truth to the human ability to harness extrasensory perception, the data is here.

As interesting as that would be to obtain, my job was to probe about their clientele, which I did. The result was 36 hours of recorded conversation with 25 psychics. Sure enough, the methodology worked. I was able to delve deeper from one conversation to the next and deliver a reliable report to the client.

For our purposes, the most relevant part happened at the beginning of the project. I was given the opportunity to try the service myself so that I could understand the customer experience. The client arranged for me to have four sessions with different psychics.

> **I seemed to have at least one cynical bone in my body.**

To be honest, I was totally skeptical. I seemed to have at least one cynical bone in my body. The client also promotes the service as "entertainment," which wasn't very reassuring. My first session reinforced those doubts. She could have guessed better than she read me. She was 25 percent accurate at best. It was less than entertaining.

The second psychic was better but still underwhelming. To my surprise, the third one was much better and interesting.

Then there was Joanie, the fourth psychic. She was extraordinary. It was creepy. She pegged me up and down, left and right. I honestly don't think she said anything wrong. Sure, there were some parts of my "read" that any cynic could cast aside as generalities, kind of like how we conform to agree with what's in our horoscopes.

Some parts were too specific to be coincidental. They were uncanny. Even so, I still view psychics and the like with skepticism, mainly because Joanie is an anomaly. However, the overall experience was convincing enough for me to believe that some of us are more gifted than others and, as such, possess an ability to make coincidences more than coincidence. Decide for yourself.

> **Start a Coincidence Journal.**

One other thing to consider, which I have not yet done personally is to start a "Coincidence Journal." Some people do something like this to study their dreams. You may find it interesting to keep tabs on your coincidences and decide which ones inspire you to follow through.

If nothing else, it's a fun excuse to see where they may lead and seek greater meaning when something incredibly outlandish occurs in our lives.

Having said all that about this mystifying yet subjective subject, you may be among those of the mindset that there's no such thing as coincidences. Fair enough. Why is that? Here's where you might say, "because everything happens for a reason." Did I get that right?

We'll explore more about causality in a little bit. What we're really talking about here is at the heart of our individual belief systems. That makes the following question somewhat rhetorical. If you don't believe in coincidences, in what do you believe?

Does everything of a coincidental nature occur because of divine intervention? Are coincidences purely a matter of quantum physics, which is to say they're proof of The Law of Attraction in action? Maybe they're the random results of the undiscovered frontier of the human brain at work.

Let's take the easy way out and concede that they're things that make you go, "hmmm."

(**February 5**) – *commentary* – above is where this chapter had come to its natural conclusion. That's no longer the case because of a fresh coincidence worth sharing on this noteworthy date.

My sister, Andrea, called me this morning to catch up having just returned from a trip. I would describe our relationship as close, but we only talk every month or two, which is about the same as with my brother, Mark. I'm almost always the one to initiate calling one another, which made it especially nice to hear from her.

Then, less than two minutes into the conversation, my brother Mark clicks in on the call-waiting. We get together for breakfast once a month with our uncle and he wanted to let me know it was rescheduled.

Without telling her who was calling, I asked my sister to hold. Just as I answered Mark, I merged the call with my sister. Suddenly, the three of us were on the phone together. None of us acknowledged the merged call and the conversation continued without missing a beat.

We chatted for a few and joked around a bit. Then the discussion turned to our brother, Dave, who would have been 57 today. Aside from the fact that Andi and Mark both called me, and at the same time, is the coincidence of it being our brother's birthday. Neither of them called for that reason. Maybe there's something subconscious to it or maybe it happened for another reason, but there's nothing that can take away from the heightened appreciation of that moment.

> *There's nothing that can take away from the heightened appreciation of that moment.*

After what happened with Dave, I'd say he was more of a taboo topic for a few years because it was too upsetting. But now we're able to speak openly about him and have a few laughs at his expense, which is what he would have wanted. We're all skilled at keeping one another humble.

> *I didn't have to wonder about what made it meaningful.*

Then we also noted how it's also our Aunt Shirley's birthday. She was my dad's only sibling. We then joked about how none of us knew how old she'd be today. As the conversation continued a bit longer, I thought to myself about how keenly aware I was of this real-time coincidence and the odds of it happening. If any one thing was certain, it's that I didn't have to wonder about what made it meaningful.

I'm very grateful to be able to share and memorialize today's unexpected experience.

This being commentary, I already had today in mind to stop writing and take the book into final edit. I've been tweaking it ad nauseum. However, this coincidence makes it easy to decide that this is the right date to stop writing. I hereby declare that the immediate fate of *Z-isms* is sealed! I may be out of time for now but do look forward to continuing the conversation in our private Reader Forum.

In any case, it would seem that, just as this part of my *Z-isms* journey takes its natural course, your journey continues on to Chapter 11 about Catching 11:11.

WOW, would you look at the time!

CHAPTER ELEVEN

Catching 11:11

As one may or may not expect about me, I can be somewhat unconventional.

When I think about my eccentricities, one that stands out is my mindfulness about catching the time 11:11 a.m. or 11:11 p.m. on a digital clock. If you're perking up right now, I know that I'm not alone about this unusual subject.

Thanks for not leaving me hanging!

But is there really something special about it? It just may be the time of day and no more significant than any other. Are we just artificially assigning meaning?

Maybe we subconsciously train ourselves to monitor our biological clocks so we're more prone to notice that special time. After all, how special can it be with 24 rotating time zones? Digital clocks are also a very recent invention in the span of human history. What's the big mystery?

Once again, can we just politely ask the cynics to zip it? At least do it for the kids!

Catching 11:11 is a common practice, especially when so many children think it's a good time to make a wish or something along those lines. Come on! Anyone who can't see the fun in that may as well skip ahead to Chapter 12.

Personally, the significance for Erica and I is our connection. We might shout, "11:11, love you!" to one another from different parts of the house. When together, it's a nice reson for an extra kiss. When apart, we're prone to do an emoji heart text with the timestamp. Yes, I admit that it is undeniably adorable. It's just one of our things that's a nice way of expressing our affection. What does 11:11 mean to you?

It may sound superstitious, but I believe the real key is to catch it spontaneously, which is to say to avoid cheating by waiting at 11:10. It's when you look at the clock for no particular reason and – BOOM – there it is! You have no idea whether it will expire in 1 or 59 seconds, but it's a moment that's however cool you choose to make it.

For me, it's a brush with that feeling of a coincidence that connects with a more conscious sense of being in the flow.

Fully tune in to the moment, even one minute can seem like a long time.

As fast as hours, days, weeks, months, seasons and years seem to fly by in our lives, catching 11:11 is also an opportunity to experience time in moments. When you stop everything and just fully tune in to the moment, even one minute can seem like a long time.

This experience also intersects with our topics about mindfulness, the value of time as a life currency and practicing gratitude as a foundation for joyfulness. It may also hold significance as an opportunity to apply to the Law of Attraction, if you subscribe to the notion that it exists.

Sometimes, especially when my wife is not within earshot, I also assign meaning to catching 11:11 to do exactly as I just described by stopping whatever I'm doing and bringing myself into that moment. It involves a certain exercise that also allows me to experiment with another force of nature.

Just go with me on this one. Here it is:

1. Upon spontaneously catching 11:11, immediately stop what you're doing, again not knowing whether seeing 11:11 has 1 or 59 seconds remaining.

2. If you're sitting or lying down, stand up and square up your feet shoulder width apart in the direction that feels most naturally faces the world, probably towards a window. Get your *Feng Shui* on.

3. The heart of this exercise is to feel the force of gravity while experiencing gratitude.

> ***Feel the force of gravity while experiencing gratitude.***

4. Focus on that singular, natural phenomenon by closing your eyes and feeling the full weight of your body underfoot. If you have never done this, you may be surprised how heavy you feel.

5. Once you allow yourself to fully connect with the force of gravity, imagine further rooting yourself beneath the surface as would a tree. If you would like to go a step further, you may find your experience can be heightened by being barefoot. How heavy can you make yourself? Concentrate.

6. With eyes still closed, turn your attention to consciously take slow, deep breaths and, after maybe 3 or 4 of them, tune into your thoughts.

7. Personally, I like to focus on a singular something for which I am grateful, usually a current aspect of my life. It might be for my health, my wife, children, family, friendships or something in the material world. It could even be about financial security or envisioning a part of my home or other places I like to visualize.

If it has to do with something I want to attract consciously, then the moment is about imagining and experiencing the feeling of already having it.

The above sequence may seem prolonged, but its purpose is to dissect the exercise, which can take as few as 10 seconds. I typically take it up to at least one minute.

The main attraction here is to experience gravity and, then, allowing it to take root. Those who identify with the Earth element may find this especially appealing. It's significant to realize your connection with gravity. It is always there, even though you are rarely aware of it. Sound familiar? Could the same be true of the Law of Attraction? What about the natural flow of energy that comprises the current?

To recap, make sure to do the exercise while intentionally feeling the force of gravity underfoot, further rooting yourself beneath the surface. Keep your eyes closed and take some conscious slow, deep breaths. Then, think of something specific for which you are extremely grateful.

So yes, it's a gratitude exercise or, in my personal experience, an opportunity. Like I said, my wife and kids already know that I can be offbeat at times. It's a quality I proudly embrace. Plus, I also like to keep them guessing!

As it happens, I had an ice hockey game a few days ago. There I was in full gear, my modern-day suit of armor. I was sitting on the bench between shifts, catching my breath, dripping sweat and I happened to look up and notice the digital clock in the rink. There it was, 11:11! You know where this is going.

I stood up on my skates, felt gravity under-blade, which was especially cool because all my weight is concentrated in the center. It was a long one. I think I caught all remaining 59 seconds, or at least it felt that way. Then I was extra ready for my next shift on the ice.

It's a pretty good use of less than a minute's worth of time. I took the opportunity to experience gratitude for feeling healthy, still playing hockey into my 50s, enjoying hanging out with the guys and the game within the game. If you play, you'll understand that one.

For what it's worth, I also take note of 10:22 p.m., when I happen to catch it. This may seem like nothing at all. However, 10:22 p.m. on a 24-hour clock is 22:22 Military Time. It's another prompt to stay mindful. I also like it as a nice reminder to honor Erica's service. It may come as no surprise that our wedding anniversary is on 11/11, which also makes Veteran's Day that much more meaningful.

Stop, stand up, take a single deep breath and think of something positive.

In and of itself, the exercise is a simple and brief meditative technique that one can do whenever and however many times a day. If you want to stretch further, next in line is either 1:11 or 5:55. It's a good reminder to pick your head up from whatever you're doing and experience that moment. At the very least, upon catching 11:11, stop, stand up, take a single deep breath and think of something positive.

Ready to give it a try? There's no need to wait. Find your spot and go for it. Again, most importantly, concentrate on your awareness of the force of gravity and feel yourself take root.

If you'd like to experiment, go for that yoga pose where you stand on one foot and sense that much more gravity. If you're able to close your eyes and still hold your position, please be sure to tell me how you do that!

Of course, the exercise is something you're free to incorporate into your daily living and an entrée to meditation and gratitude practices. When not 11:11, it's easiest to maintain by integrating into your daily routine, be that while in the shower, brushing your teeth or whenever just standing around.

Interestingly, in pulling this book together, I naturally checked out various sources from when I previously visited this topic. In this case, I found a document called "11.11 time" from 2009. It contains 19 pages of raw content, mostly from various web sources.

As I reviewed it time and time again, I realized it's fair to say that there's a broader share of opinions about what the 11:11 phenomenon means to others. The descriptions span subjects involving numerology, angelic visits, quantum physics, a "Greater Reality," and even Pagan ceremonies. Some of it seems like a whole other reality if you ask me.

It's evident that we are touching on a thoughtful topic that holds diverse meanings for a significant number of unconventional individuals. For those who join the Reader Forum, this would be one of those topics I'd love to hear more about what you and others think of the 11:11 phenomenon and any Z-isms that come into play.

Are there any other similar observances you do that involve some aspect of superstition and/or to which you assign meaning? Have you heard the one about how saying *"Rabbit, Rabbit"* first thing on the first day of a new month will bring you luck? Guilty. I've done that with Jake since he was a little boy. Erica did the same with Greta growing up, just as her mom did with her. Has this worked for anyone? It probably matters less that it means anything as much as having one more source of joy in our lives.

Suffice to say, if you weren't as tuned into 11:11 before, I feel very fortunate to have the opportunity to bring it to your attention. What meaning might it have to you?

It's less of a question of why and more one of why not.

Set your intent to try the 59-second Gratitude Exercise when you happen to catch 11:11, or at least do something you find meaningful and enjoyable. It's less of a question of why and more one of why not.

CHAPTER TWELVE

Amplifying Gratitude

☿♃

At this point, many of our topics are converging and being reinforced. Perhaps the one that intersects most among all others is the power of gratitude. We visited it in Managing Energy, Being a Life Athlete, Making Coincidences Matter, and again in Catching 11:11.

Naturally, everyone knows what gratitude is about when it comes to straightforward thankfulness in and for everyday life. Our exploration here delves into applying the well-known Law of Attraction by *Amplifying Gratitude*.

Given your interest in Z-*isms*, the odds seem pretty good that you're also someone who has studied and actively practices expressing gratitude. This likely includes having at least some awareness about one of the foremost thought leaders on this topic; that being Rhonda Byrne, author of *The Secret*.

As a champion of the Law of Attraction, Byrne specifically emphasizes gratitude as the source of magnetic power with which to connect and benefit from how the forces of energy impact our lives.

Here's one of many good excerpts from one of Ms. Byrne's ongoing supplements:

> *"Gratitude is not a mental exercise. If you simply use your mind for gratitude it will have little to no power. True gratitude comes from your heart! You must first feel it with your whole heart and radiate it from every cell.*

> *"Practice gratitude relentlessly. In a short time, your entire being will be saturated with it, and you will experience a happiness that is beyond what you can imagine. If you can really live in this highest state of gratitude, you will never have to ask for anything."*

It's easy to tell that Ms. Byrne has a distinct voice and an unbridled passion for her field of expertise. I think she got it right and continues to deliver. The rest comes down to any of us aligning and putting these natural phenomena into practice.

The less mysterious aspect of gratitude and its role in the Law of Attraction is the scientific explanation in the field of quantum physics.

It goes something like this: everything is energy. That includes you, me, our pets, and all objects, even empty space. We're talking about atoms, molecules and subatomic particles. Because of modern science, most people will accept this of solid objects like tables, chairs, walls, and the like. What they don't always realize is that their thoughts and feelings are energy as well.

> **What they don't always realize is that their thoughts and feelings are energy as well.**

As living beings, we are part of "Source Energy" in how our minds and physical beings shape the very things we perceive and encounter. This may reflect the possibility that channeling energy with the mind is the last frontier.

Everything is connected. We are living magnets. Like attracts like unto itself.

Of course, you retain the free will to be a non-believer but that still won't change that this force is always at work. If you're among those who practice religious faith, this may be second nature. A lot of people pray which, by no coincidence, also mirrors practices that harness the Law of Attraction.

If so many human beings subscribe to their belief in a higher power, most commonly regarded as G-d, might it stand to reason that the Law of Attraction is something we're able to influence with a similar faith? This is a sensitive subject to say the least. Please know that my intentions here are wholly respectful.

One of the individuals featured in *The Secret*, James Arthur Ray, conveyed an interesting perspective along these lines:

"Most people define themselves by this finite body, but you're not a finite body. Even under a microscope you're an energy field."

He then compared the scientific explanation about what created the universe between how a quantum physicist might describe energy versus how a theologian might describe G-d. The descriptions are almost identical, as follows:

"[It] always [existed] and always will. [It] can never be created or destroyed. [It is] always moving into form, through form and out of form."

His point is that we are all spiritual beings and energy fields that operate in a larger energy field.

Energy attracts like energy.

Energy attracts like energy. All forms of matter and energy are attracted to that of like vibration. Synchronizing one's vibration with attraction and using gratitude as an amplifier will align with that experience.

If you're someone who can wrap your head around this enough to fully understand, more power to you. I just gave that explanation my best shot, which was an easy reminder that I am not a quantum physicist.

However, it matters less to understand it than it is to be aware and just accept that it is one of the forces of nature, like gravity. Honestly, it goes beyond surface-level acceptance to be more about one's belief. At the very least, consider being open to the possibility.

Many of today's most incredible scientific truths were met with ridicule by skeptics and naysayers who chose to cling to their old way of thinking, regardless of the fact that it was just plain wrong.

The truth is what it is.

Even if this energy-attraction stuff has yet to resonate for you, a little bit of reasoning will show it is ultimately up to us to interpret our experiences. It does not matter if we see them as good, bad or something different. The truth is what it is.

This also directly links back to perception and how different people can experience the same situation in very different ways. Our discussion on mood management intersects here as well.

Looking back at our perspective about applying Earned Confidence, this also raises the stakes about the toxicity of unnecessary worry and anxiety. Now combine that with the principles of the Law of Attraction. What if the reason something you worried about actually happens because of your worry and expectation for it to occur? Ironically, your energy may be the origin of that self-fulfilling prophecy.

Ironically, your energy may be the origin of that self-fulfilling prophecy.

The cycle worsens when you think you were right to worry in the first place, which reinforces that behavior. It's one thing to have this apply to something about yourself. However, what if you're worrying about someone else attracts that negative consequence and causes it to affect them? That may seem a bit extreme, but is it?

Accepted as fact, this also means the life circumstances that are occurring right now represent a residual reflection of our past thoughts and actions. We must also factor the energy exchanges with other individuals in our life orbit. They may interact and affect how we think and feel in similar manners as referenced earlier in our discussion about Managing Energy. There's a lot to it. We need to take charge!

Whether you are aware of it or not, you are attracting people, situations, opportunities and much more into your life. Hopefully, now that you are more mindful of this Law and how it works, you can start to use it to deliberately attract what you want into your life.

> **What you expect, tends to happen.**

Whatever we expect has a greater tendency and likelihood to occur. You can shorten that by saying, "what you expect, tends to happen."

If there is any single line to take away from this entire book, that could be it. The obvious thing to wonder is if it can be that simple. If you become aware of them and zero in on your expectations, you can control your personal destiny. Align your expectations with your desires once you are clear about them.

Our innate will is always active in what we choose and how those choices make us feel. You're either going to continue to attract by default, or you can choose to work at this and create a life you intentionally desire.

Most people want to attract money, success and things like that. Yet most of the time they are worrying about money and success while complaining about how difficult things are. What do you think they will attract? That's right, more things to worry and complain about. If that happens to be your mindset, then stop the cycle! Even if that point stands on its own apart from the topic of attraction, those habits are vital to break.

When we think with intention and concentrate on what it is we want, which means enjoying it as if it were here already, our energy vibration aligns with that frequency to attract whatever it is we desire.

One of the first things you can do to get to this place is to be grateful for what you already have in your life. Include all things in this gratitude because all of it has led you to the point where you will begin to amplify that attraction consciously.

I am a work in progress just like you.

Let's share some tough love for a moment. Having the discipline to do and sustain all of this is anything but easy. Personally, I cannot claim to have mastered it. I am a work in progress just like you. The challenge is akin to mustering the motivation and consistency to maintain an exercise routine.

Nonetheless, I do give partial credit for my life upgrades in recent years to practicing visualization and Amplifying Gratitude. I cannot claim to have done a formal vision board or anything yet, but I have stayed crystal clear about my vision and expectations.

In 2013, I hit a very low point. Let's just say that I got myself in a massive hole that few people believed I could ever dig out, let alone continue to push forward once I did manage to escape. There was no other way to go but up.

It's natural to experience two or three steps forward and one back. That's life. Just stay consistent, keep the math in your favor and you'll make it happen.

Fast forward to today. I dug out of that hole and am well on my way to climbing the mountain. I truly feel that I am living my best life right now and that even better times lie ahead. I met and married my soulmate. Each of us added an amazing teenager to our combined family. We've built our dream home, have made some amazing new friends and even adopted three Bengal cats (Buzz, Paizley and Zoey). It's a zoo, but they're a lot of fun. We continue to earn our security and appreciate our freedom.

> *I try to focus my energies on experiencing moments in real time.*

I try to focus my energies on experiencing moments in real time, recognizing that I spend most days with the flexibility to make my own schedule and working at my home office. Erica does the same. I take gratitude breaks, though I would benefit from doing more.

I am incredibly grateful for being healthy and able to do the many things I love with my family and for myself. I still enjoy playing ice hockey and riding the motorcycle on country roads. Now I have the opportunity to publish my first book and to positively impact as many other people as possible.

The point of this disclosure is that 2013 is the year that I set my sights on the life I have now. It wasn't just about wishful thinking or the Law of Attraction by itself. A lot had to happen. It took me about three years to unbury. Once again, there was no other way but through.

YOUR TURN TO SUCCEED

Now it's your turn. Take stock. Begin with what matters most: being alive, the love in your life, friendships and having your basic needs met. Start to consider your *why*.

If there is any single motive that draws people to channel gratitude, it's probably to attract wealth and other forms of abundance. Sure, go for it! It's okay. Get materialistic.

Consider doing a vision board and focusing intently on those desires. How does it make you feel in the present tense? How does your life change as a result? Discover the answers for yourself.

Another thing you might try is flipping through a department store circular and identifying all the things you want versus those you really need. Chances are that there are very few to none of the latter, which is to say you have already achieved a level of abundance. That's a solid reason to experience gratitude mindfully.

While that's a worthy example, it's only a one-time thing. The key to Amplifying Gratitude is to create habits and, with it, turn everyday experiences into enriching ones. A very simple exercise might be to replace, "Today, I have to _____," with "Today, I *get* to _____." Think of it as a gratitude converter.

> *Turn everyday experiences into enriching ones.*

A simple approach is to repurpose your downtime while waiting in line. If it's about going to the grocery store, then instead of feeling annoyed about how slow the check-out person is moving, use those minutes to look in your cart, be grateful for each item and then do the same as you place them on the conveyor belt.

Let's say you have to stop by the pharmacy drive-through and you're two cars back. Take a moment to convert your impatience into gratitude by thinking and feeling how awesome it is that modern science has produced something to make you or a loved one feel better. Then, as the clerk finishes the transaction, be sure to look them in the eye and express appreciation.

You can even try it for chores around the house. There's everything right about feeling grateful for clean laundry, having a neat home and fresh cat litter. Did you notice that I used the opposite term instead of saying, "there's nothing wrong?" Yes, try to catch yourself when you use negative terms and convert them. Rather than be someone who hedges by saying, "I don't disagree with you," it's noticeably better to simply say, "I agree with you." The person to whom you say that will surely agree.

This all may seem silly at first, but at least it helped you be less impatient in store lines and less annoyed about household tasks, which are great reasons to be grateful all by themselves. Correction, I meant to say, "more patient" and "more pleasant." Even the slightest shift in routine activities and conversations will enrich your experiences and make you a kinder person to be around as well as to yourself.

> *No matter far you've gone in the wrong direction, you can always turn around.*

It's a wonderful life after all. If not, it still can be. No matter how long or far you've gone in the wrong direction, you can always turn around. One decision can change your life.

As mentioned, even those deprived of abundance can find their own. Again, somewhere on Earth in some poverty-stricken third world country, there's someone who enjoys much greater inner happiness than someone in a developed country with great wealth whose spirit and sense of self are broken.

If you are among those who have practiced meditation, yoga or a martial art that underscores the importance of quieting the mind, then you've gained an advantage. Taking it a step further, as they do in *The Secret*, is the practice of pinpointing future desires and attracting them into the present by experiencing them as if you already have them. This may be why Einstein emphasized imagination.

Just to reiterate, when something vibrates at a certain frequency, it naturally resonates with and attracts things with the same frequency. We will attract into our experience that with which we are vibrationally synchronous. It also gives added meaning to those who believe in sending good vibes and among those who are open to receiving them.

> *Gratitude will accelerate you through your growth and amplify success.*

Gratitude will accelerate you through your growth and amplify success more than just about any amount of hard work.

It almost seems more credible, if not more practical. There's also a lot to be said for the power of visualization. When we seek to put our beliefs into action by applying the Law of Attraction, there are specific techniques to follow.

1. Get very clear on what you want.

2. Visualize and raise your vibration about it.

3. Allow it.

4. Take inspired action.

You must be very clear and precise about your desire. Focus on it. Give it all your positive energy. Feel good!

> **You must be very clear and precise about your desire.**

It's understandable if your first reaction is that you're not a light switch that can just turn on all those good feelings and positive energy. Okay, what are some things you can apply to amplify your gratitude? It may be as simple as holding a meaningful object or listening to a favorite song to give you a lift. What brings you joy? Make a conscious effort to pet and play with your pet and be in that moment. Dogs and cats exude positive energy. It seems less certain about turtles, gerbils or fish. Yet, if those are the pets that bring you joy, it's your passion that matters.

What internal stimuli can you incorporate? Is there someone you hold in your heart that you can call upon for strength? How about a close family member who has passed on?

Another example, which may sound corny to some, is to go to your happy place and take a tour. If you've yet to know where that is, it's usually easy to think of somewhere from your past or a current treasured destination, be that a certain beach or mountain.

For me, it's that ice hockey camp in Northern Ontario that I referenced earlier. It's been almost 40 years since I was there, but I often mentally revisit it and recall so much detail of the physical property. It doesn't seem so far away. It also helps me reconnect and better hold on to the good memories I made there.

> *Be in tune with the natural forces that attract what is in harmony with yourself.*

Any thought you may have, when combined with emotion, vibrates out from you to the universe and will attract back what you want. Experience what it feels like to envision the image of the world you want in your life. This energy moves much like an ocean. As energetic beings, this exercise is about controlling your vibration so that you will be in tune with the natural forces that attract what is in harmony with yourself.

You may also come face-to-face with your own self-defeating mindset and destructive behavior. It's essential to believe that you deserve what you want, that you can have it, that it's possible for you and that you can let it unfold. Keep this top of mind.

It's also vital to remain true to yourself as you experience push-back from external forces and events. In short, be clear about how to not get knocked off your game and, if that does happen, what you must do to get back on track.

More specifically, as you focus more on Amplifying Gratitude and aligning your vibration with what you want to attract, it becomes more likely that others around you may react negatively. It may even be subconscious whereby others sense something in you and their own dysfunctions take hold.

I share this with you because I've experienced such interferences in experimenting with the Law of Attraction. There may be Spiders or others who are simply unable to control their insecurities.

> *There may be Spiders or others who are simply unable to control their insecurities.*

Free yourself. Stop worrying about what other people think and letting that affect your behavior. If their negative impact doesn't let up, then it's another indicator to insulate this relationship or sever it altogether.

Be aware enough to remain objective and, rather than be drained by others' negativity, rely on your empathy, compassion and pride in knowing that what you're doing is working.

> *Positive energy can bring us more of what we want in our lives.*

This framework about how positive energy can bring us more of what we want in our lives also raises the importance of applying Earned Confidence to ward off worry and anxiety. It's a fine line between keeping yourself from expecting something undesired and being prepared to repel it.

We all encounter challenges and difficult obstacles we need to overcome. What matters is that we convert such events into opportunities to become stronger. Distractions are going to come. You'll need to expend energy to handle those situations and not lose focus.

One of the examples in *The Secret* that I really like refers to imagining oneself driving at night and trusting that, although your headlights only illuminate the next 200 feet, the following stretch of road is there and reveals itself with progress. Whether it's one step or one mile at a time, just keep moving forward.

> *Be open to living your life by design and design it.*

As your life takes shape and you begin to see the link between your thoughts and your experiences, you become a deliberate thinker. You no longer think negatively, cast doubts or hold rigid preferences. Be open to living your life by design and design it.

It's also essential to consider that the benefits of practicing gratitude may not work as well in a vacuum. It also needs to align and draw its power from other topics we have covered that include:

- Experiencing life in the moment
- Loving oneself
- Applying Earned Confidence
- Harnessing inner strength
- Having compassion for others
- Refusing to internalize negative energy
- Minimizing stress
- Positively interacting with others
- Perceiving events optimistically
- Making meaningful connections
- Having a strong Tribe
- Forgiving your regrets
- Embracing and practicing personal growth
- Maintaining a sense of comfort, peace and harmony within oneself

Okay, that's *a lot* of alignment, but you get the idea.

You may find it helpful to focus on any one of the above topics at a time, such as by between chapters and whenever else you can amplify gratitude.

Bringing the above inner forces into alignment is also likely to heighten your ability to apply another amplifier, which is giving. The key to effective giving includes staying open to receiving. Givers attract. Be magnetic. This may also strengthen your influence, which is determined by how abundantly you place other people's interests first.

Putting it all together, it can seem beyond overwhelming and, as such, discouraging. Take a breath. Make that a few conscious, deep breaths. When you step back, hopefully the fact is that most everything is generally okay. So, take heart. *You're still standing!*

> *When you step back, hopefully the fact is that most everything is generally okay.*

You may have noticed some redundancies throughout our exploration of Amplifying Gratitude. I hope you can appreciate that these were by design to reinforce the most salient points to put into practice. We'll revisit these some more as we wind down.

Given the high stakes involving our happiness and fulfillment, it seems worth the effort to experiment with gratitude and see what happens.

CHAPTER THIRTEEN

Inevitability

We've definitely come through our share of complexities to explore Amplifying Gratitude to fuel attraction. After all, its square root is derived from quantum physics. That's a daunting topic by itself.

If we think of the Law of Attraction as a practice and process for what perpetually shapes our lives, then the intent to dive even deeper into Inevitability is more about our destination for what we know to be our purpose. In essence, it's about our *why*.

As such, as we explore Inevitability, one aspect of which I'm certain is that it is surely the most complicated topic in the book. So if you've been reading for a while, just do a check-in with yourself and affirm that you have enough gas in the tank to go another round.

My motive for this suggestion is to achieve the goal for you to get the most out of the book and the practical insights you take away and put into action. Let's get to it!

When you think of Inevitability, does anything come to mind

that you wholeheartedly believe or know will happen? Hold that thought while we attempt to pinpoint what Inevitability means for our purposes.

One way of looking at it is being so absolutely certain that something will occur that it represents the equivalent of something that has already happened, except in the future. This may well be the most closed loop way of interpreting an inevitable eventuality, but that's also precisely the point.

This goes beyond Amplifying Gratitude by visualizing already having something in the present. It's not about imagination as much as it is an undeterrable belief. To help us out, here's the conventional definition from Mr. Webster:

Inevitability
(Noun) in·ev·i·ta·bil·ity
[in-ev-i-t*uh*-b*uh*-l-eh-tee]

> *That which is unable to be avoided, evaded,*
> *or escaped; certain; necessary; sure to occur,*
> *happen, or come; unalterable.*

One interesting observation about the word inevitable is that it's a common thread in the definitions of fate, destiny and Karma, among others.

> *It's not about imagination as much as it is an undeterrable belief.*

Let's hit the reset button and start anew with what Inevitability is not. There are small things that are readily achievable that we make happen in the short-term. These are items we might have on our to-do lists that we check off in a matter of hours, days, weeks and months. Those items are off this table.

It's also safe to say that our examples about being in the flow and coincidences, such as those perfect seats, spaces and car rides are more about personal manifestations. They are also hit or miss.

More significant examples of this would be finding the perfect house you're seeking with relatively minimal effort. Things happen that feel effortless or even serendipitous. They may even be wholly coincidental. These, too, are more about personal energy and alignment, which I think you'll find we have well-covered.

When we consider Inevitability, it applies to very specific events or significant personal goals in which we fully believe and are totally committed to make happen. They are *our* inevitabilities. Of course, all of this must be within reason and conceptually achievable.

> *Inevitability, it's more about eventualities that are effortful.*

Once again, being in the flow and manifesting material things by experiencing them as almost effortless is something else. As we explore the topic of Inevitability, it's more about eventualities that are *effortful*.

For our purposes, the main power source for defining and achieving Inevitability is specific to us as individual human beings. It is energy-driven, fueled by ones' crystal-clear vision about that eventuality. It's about purpose and your *why*. Along with all of that must come a combination of willfulness, tenacity, grit, passion, belief and, ultimately, the full degree of faith in ourselves. Think of it as compulsory. Consider yourself unstoppable.

There's nothing quite like necessity to make something happen.

Actualizing an Inevitability may also involve great personal sacrifice, such as financial hardship that falls in the category of "doing whatever it takes." The expression "do or die trying" also comes to mind. Here's also where Earned Confidence is essential. Naturally, it's more ideal when ones' sacrifices are less extreme.

In the balance is that we are energy beings. We also have an innate need to be useful, to achieve, to create, to be challenged, to contribute and to have meaningful goals that lead to purposeful accomplishments that bring us true fulfillment.

An Inevitability is bigger in the context of whatever that means to the person. It's about total alignment as it relates to high-level aspirations. Yes, in the example of relationships, the Inevitability of meeting your soulmate can qualify. Of course, you must first believe that your soulmate exists. Our skeptics might call them ideally compatible individuals and that there are "plenty of fish in the sea." Do you think they're right?

The front end of the equation for Inevitability might begin by setting an intention to encounter a romantic interest that you see yourself wanting to meet. That's straightforward. However, here we are surely channeling gratitude and the Law of Attraction. Then it happens somewhat effortlessly in a flow-like manner, such as both experiencing love at first sight. Has that happened for you? Not so fast. We are still at the manifestation stage. That amazing relationship still has its honeymoon period.

The Inevitability of that person truly being your soulmate still comes down to putting in the work to turn it into something long-term. It still involves normal relationship challenges and settling into a certain groove where your love still holds strong. It's when you both know you have reached that destination that Inevitability is assured by the "'til death do us part" statement. Some of us might call that an accepted marriage proposal while others wait for the second ring. I think most of us will agree that relationships can be effortful, for better or for worse.

 As we look at the big picture and our overall life aspirations, it's essential to step back and get as clear as possible, especially about things that may take years to achieve. One of the best ways that I have found to pinpoint an Inevitability is to break it down by visualizing dominos. When people begin to formulate goals, the natural tendency is to evaluate their current status in relation to that goal. They see themselves at Point A. Then they do what they think they need to do to work

towards achieving that goal, which they view as Point B. Ideally, they can fully define both points and may even develop a formal plan of action to get from here to there.

Once you strategize, place the last domino first.

However, when we become crystal clear about a goal, especially the really big and most relevant ones, that plan of action will be a straighter line by drawing it from Point B as the starting point, then backwards to Point A. In other words, once you strategize, place the last domino first. In a sense, by eliminating at least some randomness, this makes it possible to fold time by envisioning, focusing on and expecting that inevitable outcome.

Now's a good time to refer to the credible logic of Malcolm Gladwell with his book and mainstreamed phrase, *The Tipping Point*. By definition, this does not refer to your first domino at your current Point A. The actual tipping point refers to the specific domino that is somewhere along the line that, once tipped, makes certain the remaining dominos between that location and Point B will continue to fall until that Inevitability fully comes to fruition.

This fact offers much needed and immense encouragement for those who envision an eventuality of something so massive that it will assuredly take many years to achieve. We will not even bother to calculate the amount of energy it would take for that momentum to exponentially evolve beyond what one would currently envision or possess.

More specifically, that domino also represents an axis point where, once reached, the rest will continue to fall into place.

A common example of this would be the aspiration of an entrepreneur of any start-up company. They have a business plan with goals set at years 1, 3, 5, 10 and perhaps beyond. The common tipping point here is the domino that represents sustainable profitability. After all, once their business model stabilizes, they will be able to hire the next two people, then four, and then eight.

Essentially, they are at the point of never looking back.

I would like to share a key point to prevent you from sabotaging or giving up on your goals. You would do well to refrain from countering the thought of arriving at such a tipping point with unsubstantiated, defeating variables like competition, technology advances or consumer demand. In other words, it's fine to factor those potential challenges and obstacles into your official business plan, but the core focus to pursue your Inevitability in this context is to disregard barriers. This falls into the same category of worry and anxiety attracting those unwanted events.

Most importantly, even if you place your dominos in perfect order in a straight line from Point B back to Point A, making it happen still relies on your crystallized vision, willpower, dedication, and even a level of intrinsic faith and expectation in the Inevitability you seek to actualize.

This is also why the nucleus of that power is you knowing your purpose, your *why*, that will supply inexhaustible fuel to drive your unwavering passion that brings your Inevitability to fruition.

> **The nucleus of that power is you knowing your purpose, your why.**

Some people go their whole lives without questioning who they are, whether they have a sense of purpose in life and how to fulfill it. Others become mired in codependency and never individualize their perspective and effort. It's essential to confront these barriers to success just the same.

So how might you identify a Point B that's worthy of such effort and sacrifice? Admittedly, that's a tough one, especially given everyone's uniqueness. One thing to consider is confronting the ultimate Inevitability.

Ask yourself a couple of pointed questions.

If you could go back and change one thing, what would it be? What would you do differently? This isn't about rehashing regret as much as it is to see whether the answer can have a positive impact now. Similarly, if you were to jump to the end of your life, what are the three most important lessons you will have wanted to learn? Why are they so critical? Reflect on one or two things that you know you will deeply regret if you do not make them happen. Is preventing that regret enough to become your *why?* Are the things you identify still achievable?

Writing this book is the direct result of me asking myself that confrontational question. I've had it in me for at least 15 years and, although writing it before now would have been premature, it was among my top 3 potential regrets. Prevention achieved! Are you among the many others who think and talk about writing a book? Is there some other creation you have yet to manifest? What about factoring your kids and their kids into the equation? How about your legacy?

Here's a less than comfortable way to discover and/or confirm our *why?* If we were to skip ahead to our ultimate Point B, that being our life's end, how would we want our obituary to read? Notice how that's written in the third person. Less morbidly, focus less upon anything negative and stick with those big life goals. Then narrow them down to those that would fulfill any facets of your *why.*

Some people may not find it as easy to discover their purpose, but they have a broader goal, such as achieving a certain degree of financial accomplishment. Start there. If I'm not mistaken, it's a well-documented fact that the predominant common thread among millionaires, putting all variables aside, is that they *believed* they would be millionaires.

Let's experiment with that notion for a moment. Put yourself in that mindset and approach it with a level of faith. You wholeheartedly believe and expect, in every fiber of yourself, that you are a millionaire in the not-too-distant future. In this way, our mindset may be our most valuable asset.

Aside from the long odds of the lottery, what could possibly occur for that to happen? What direction might that take? Let's say you still don't know. How about we step back and begin with Amplifying Gratitude. How does it feel to be a millionaire now? What kind of life are you experiencing? Turn the kaleidoscope. Put yourself there and then stick with it.

In any case, it's a healthy exercise to think through. It might also serve as a vetting process to be certain your desire to make something inevitable exists or not. Of course, that's okay. This all comes down to free will, which is entirely respectable.

Ultimately, each of us will want to design our lives and dictate how we expend energy in relation to our personal values. Think about it. What is it that you already love about your life? Are there aspects that you find incredibly fulfilling? We have covered this quite a bit, but reinforcement is good for what matters most.

> *Successful people are those who are good at doing the things they don't like to do.*

This is a good place to share a *Z-ism* by someone I know – Successful people are those who are good at doing the things they don't like to do. Is that an insight to live by?

More often than not, the more activities, people and time that are spent in alignment with your values, the more fulfilled you will be. As a result, ask yourself which achievements bring you the highest level of satisfaction.

You might also find that you are coming up blank and trying to set your sights on desired inevitabilities that seem too big a proposition. That's okay, too. It also makes sense to start small and remain present by identifying 3 to 5 values and, then, 1 to 3 ways you can honor each value every week or every day.

You'll find some activities can honor many of your values simultaneously. Integrate these activities into your life. Make room for new activities by eliminating less-fulfilling ones and energy drains. As discussed, this may include spending less time with certain people. Start there and keep it simple. Again, experience such things in real-time to create momentum and bring more fulfillment into your life.

That said, once you find a purpose worthy of Inevitability, there's a delicate balance to achieve alignment between living in the moment and visualizing that future. This takes us back to Amplifying Gratitude by experiencing future desires in the present, if only through imagination.

It's also not enough to visualize. There may be certain skills that require effortful commitment to acquire. What might those be for you? How will you hone them? In the likelihood that you cannot achieve something alone, the next question could relate to building your network. Who specifically might you need to know and how might you cultivate those relationships? Once clear, don't wait!

It seems like we're at the point of covering the conceptual part about this topic reasonably well and are ready to delve into actual examples. Since our focus on Inevitability is specific to an individual, this also requires a final round of personal disclosure. I have no precise frame of reference other than my own and I am most grateful to have the opportunity to share more with you.

It's tempting to get into the backstory of how I met Erica, how we experienced love at first sight and it all working out with us knowing we truly are soulmates. That may seem a little too personal of an example, but I can attest that our meeting and how we are together resulted from mutual manifestation.

There's also the obvious example of publishing this book, which I have known for some time is among the more notable inevitabilities in my life. Some of the topics, including this one, have been well-established for many years. However, it hasn't been until now that it felt right to complete and do what it takes to get it published. Are you ready to write your book? An even better question is who said that being ready is a prerequisite?

In my case, a key factor of this timing has been a matter of accumulating life experiences, greater maturity and the confidence to put this out there. I finally have enough seasoning. Another major factor has to do with earning the life currency that I value most. For me, earning my freedom affords me the time and personal energy to put in the work. So here it is: *Z-isms* has come to fruition!

This chapter would be incomplete if we didn't acknowledge the unavoidable inevitabilities in our lives. There's the old adage about the certainty of death and taxes. Everyone in America knows about April 15th. Our time limit is another matter.

For instance, Erica and I have a very good friend who is battling Stage 4 prostate cancer. It is incurable. All medical science can do for the time being is prolong his life. Of all things, they just found out his wife has Stage 1 breast cancer and needs a double mastectomy. Yet both of them are among the most positive people we know. Come to think of it, they're also the most courageous and gracious people I have ever met. We try to get together often and embrace the opportunity to have the best time together.

What if any of us learned that we had an incurable health condition that limited our remaining time, how would that change our approach to our remaining life? This may include having the quality of it degrade severely the closer we got to the end. This example is too negative to personalize but remains essential.

> ***Think about it but be objective as if you were role-playing for someone else.***

Think about it but be objective as if you were role-playing for someone else. The reason for that approach regards what we just covered about not emitting any energy to attract anything undesired upon ourselves. Don't chance it.

I grew up as close as one gets to a similar tragedy. My mom had a routine surgery sometime in the early '80s before the blood supply was better screened. She inherited the unfortunate distinction of being among the first heterosexual women to contract the Human Immunodeficiency Virus, or HIV.

Worse yet, the stigma was so bad at the time that she kept it from me and my brothers and sister for nearly two more years until she became more symptomatic. The stigma about AIDS was at its worst at that time and my mom truly feared that we would disown her. It wells me up. I can't even imagine what that was like for her. We knew something was wrong but the actual news naturally came as a surprise. Of course, we all rallied around her and gave our full love and support.

Today, medical science has advanced treatments to control the virus for people to live long and healthy lives, which seems miraculous. My mom's remaining years were just the opposite. She got the worst of it.

We did everything we could to keep her spirits up and make the most of our time together. We did everything we could to keep her spirits up and make the most of our time together. It was hard. It didn't help that she had bouts of depression on top of all else. She was in and out of hospitals and we thought we'd lose her any number of times. She somehow made it another 13 years, though her faculties severely diminished.

Toward the end, her dementia was as bad as it gets. However, she loved movies and there were 5 or 6 that she could watch one day to the next as if seeing them for the first time. I've seen *Sleepless in Seattle* dozens of times, among others. There's no way around the fact that it was harrowing. We knew we'd lose her and she knew she'd lose herself. But we all made the best of it together. There was no other way but through.

It's safe to say that some of my inspiration for the book comes from having to cope with something so extreme for so long and being a caregiver.

Thank you, Mom. You're *always* in my heart.

Everything about a terminal illness is reactively proactive, be it with healthcare or making the remaining time matter most. The reality is also that, regardless of how healthy we are, life is naturally terminal. I hope sharing this encourages you and others to be more preventative with self-care and proactive with making the most of your one go-round.

Another example of Inevitability I'd like to share is about my day job running The Internship Institute, which I founded to address critical problems and create meaningful opportunities.

> *True to our mission, we are "Making Experience Matter"*

True to our mission, we are "Making Experience Matter" by setting up and fixing internship programs. The reason we focus on employers is that internships can't matter if the programs don't exist. In addition, if they are less than worthwhile, internships have a negative impact and are more likely to cease to exist.

We sometimes refer to this as "Internship Installations" or that we "Johnny Appleseed" programs. In any case, it's been at least 10 times more challenging than I ever imagined. It easily makes the cut as an example of swimming against the current and stands above all else in not following my own advice to change directions.

The question I get more than any other is about what got me into it. But the one that matters most is about what keeps me going.

What's my *why?* Sure, after about 25,000+ hours, significant personal investment and immeasurable sacrifice, it's partly that I have come too far not to see it through. The most important reason is what's at stake. I know of no one else who can do it.

If not me, then who? I have a responsibility.

We've developed programs that started off with 2 students that have expanded over time to now providing 50+ intern opportunities year after year. Is it too grandiose to believe that internships are a means to revive the American Dream?

> *If not me, then who? I have a responsibility.*

Have you ever seen the movie, *The Pursuit of Happyness* with Will Smith? It's about the real-life rags-to-riches story of Chris Gardner, a single dad who lifted himself and his young son out of poverty to become a financial broker. He proved himself through an internship that became his springboard to continue his upward mobility. He knew his *why*. He did it. His hard work and sheer determination made success inevitable.

Some of our work creates similar stepping stones for disadvantaged youth and military veterans. I believe my responsibility to accomplish the mission of the nonprofit is far greater because the vision that drives it is much bigger than setting up and fixing internship programs. More specifically, there's a systemic plan to physically build the talent pipeline in the form of regional job placement and skills training hubs.

At the systemic level, internships become a catalyst to remedy some of our most daunting societal problems. The challenge here has less to do with fixing a system that's broken than it does with building a system that does not exist.

The reason for sharing this in such detail is to illustrate how achieving something so massive takes more than one man on a mission with a vision and steadfast belief to make inevitable.

This leads us to another consult with Malcolm Gladwell and his work with *Outliers*. Among his principal findings was that it takes at least 10,000 hours for an individual to attain mastery and momentum. The other and even more critical factor is that it is next to impossible to achieve lofty goals by going it alone. That part is typically much more difficult to make happen.

He's right. In fact, no matter what I can do on my own, there are three essential missing ingredients. Money surely tops the list, mostly to fund the second which is manpower. In our case, it's to hire U.S. veterans transitioning from active duty. They possess the transferable skills to do what we do. At least as vital is the third ingredient, which is the muscle of those with the power and influence to remove and break through the many barriers in our way.

One cannot do with what one does not have.

Unfortunately, there's no such thing as venture capital investors for nonprofits. If we were a start-up company, we'd aim to raise about $2 million to build capacity to get under our own power.

Our cause is also too obscure to attract public donations. I may not have the exact answer now, but my belief in the mission is unwavering and my determination remains undeterred. What if I were to actualize the notion that the proceeds from this book will fund the nonprofit? What if someone reading this very sentence has the curiosity, wherewithal and a philanthropic mindset to contact me and make it happen?

OUR MODEL

We hire veterans
to train employers and recruit interns

Our veterans help employers
set up successful internship programs

Those internships create job opportunities
for veterans and others in work transition

From here forward remains a much more detailed business plan that is too involved to share. Trusting that you take my word for it, let's stay on topic about the importance of having that crystal clear vision, as your Point B and how to work backwards from that inevitable eventuality to bring it into being.

Optimistically, the nonprofit can reach its current Point B within approximately 50 years. We're talking about job placement and training hubs in nearly every county nationwide. The good news is that we won't have to wait that long to make it inevitable. In fact, hurdles aside, the actual axis of our tipping point is remarkably close. We're talking about the domino we need to reach to make the rest fall, which is to achieve commercial sustainability.

Put another way, once we hire our first four veterans to serve as our TrainingCorps of internship program recruiters, trainers, installers and certifiers, the revenue they generate not only secures their own incomes but enables us to hire our next four veterans. The momentum will continue exponentially to Point B and beyond.

Wait, what if the all-important domino is the idea to develop something that makes it possible to achieve commercial sustainability? What if it's the concerted effort to Amplify Gratitude that attracts the inspiration to spawn the idea? Do you see where this is going? Could a new Point A have been four paragraphs ago when I invited those who can help to contact me?

Any one of the dominos above could tip the next 50+ years of progress. Though I know it's far from achieveable alone, the current fate of The Internship Institute remains squarely within my willpower.

Eventually, everything therein converges to become an inevitable manifestation.

As daunting as it may sound, there's a simplicity to it that travels along the same lines as the Law of Attraction, which plays a central role to Inevitability. Set a goal, focus your intent on a fixed point, align your expectations and energy and declare that fixed vision as already achieved. Eventually, everything therein converges to become an inevitable manifestation.

Personally, I can't claim to have given my very best effort to apply and amplify the Law of Attraction to fully actualize an Inevitability of this magnitude. But if there was any time worth giving it a try, it's now with this book.

Writing and publishing *Z-isms* has gotten me this far. But what good is the book if it doesn't gain traction? The purpose driving this Inevitability is to positively impact as many people as possible. Could the book release be the tipping point? I'm not sure that's a reasonable expectation. There's work to be done. Books don't promote themselves. This isn't about marketing. That's transactional.

It's going to take more than just making a list and doing a vision board. I need to get crystal clear about my Point B, that future reality and the expectations to step into it.

My newfound belief is in the book itself and it being a vehicle for exponential good. At the very least, my newfound belief is in the book itself and it being a vehicle for exponential good. That happening, by default, makes me a known author.

As I get clearer about the specific domino in my endeavors that represents Point B, how much closer can I envision another domino beyond then and further straighten and shorten the full line? For example, replacing the word "known" with "famous" would mean pushing Point B further out. For this to reconcile, does that mean I need to shift the paradigm about my self-identity and try to experience life as already being a famous author?

At this moment, if I'm envisioning the utmost Inevitability for *Z-isms* and my future identity, one thought is to believe and expect that Matt Zinman is *already* a household name. It's just that the houses don't know it yet. Is that my destiny, my fate, my path, my reality and/or my ambition? That matters less than having the self-belief that the book will have that massive ripple effect.

How do I manage this self-image paradigm-shift? It's by staying true to myself and trusting my gut. There are some natural feelings of apprehension, especially with respect to my own sense of self and coming from a true place of authenticity, humility and gratitude.

What if I alter my inner monologue to believe and behave as if, every day from now on that I am, here and now, what one would consider to be a famous author? Will that make it more possible to bring that to fruition? Is it worth the try? Can I just step into it? My highest priority is to stay grounded, remain true to myself and never let anything go to my head.

Our experiences and our ambitions shape our identities.

For me, it's a moment of knowing that our experiences and our ambitions shape our identities. Thinking about it, as I see and experience the effects of my writing the book, I can recognize and more-naturally experience myself as this well-regarded author. Okay, where does that leave me? Better yet, where does that lead me?

Thinking this through while still working on this part of the book, I've begun to experiment with shifting my perspective about that being a new reality. In fact, getting clearer about my new *why* and mission moving forward has enabled me to reverse engineer some of the final points throughout the book.

Specifically, it allowed me to look back and see things from the vantage point of that famous author guy and view things now from that future perspective. I wish all this were simple and easy, but then it wouldn't be effortful.

See if you can identify which domino in the sequence is the actual tipping point.

Given the complexities of this particular subject, let's wrap up by reinforcing the key point to making an achievable outcome inevitable. Draw your Point B to Point A and back to the point of origin. Maintain an unwavering, full expectation that you will make it happen. See if you can identify which domino in the sequence is the actual tipping point. Then *show up* for work.

CHAPTER FOURTEEN

Winning the Battle Within

There's no way to know how many people have ever viewed themselves as their own worst enemy. My guess is that the percentage is sadly high. Hopefully, that's not currently the case for you.

Naturally, nobody knows that enemy better than ourselves. The key factor comes back to there being no substitute for experience and our being the only ones in our own heads.

What is it that goes so wrong in our lives that we reach the point of seeing ourselves as the enemy? Self-destruction aside, this is probably too soon to ask that big of a question. Let's change the subject for now and start small by looking at other than our innermost thoughts.

What if you could eliminate complaining from your life? First, there's that one thing you have control over: your behavior. As a refresher, let's go back to our example of being out with friends and that restaurant server in a bad mood. It may seem justified to complain. After all, they're getting paid to serve you and the customer is always right. Right?

What good will come of that approach? Will that make you feel better? What if you made a conscious decision to be empathetic about their having a bad day? Better yet, you go out of your way to make them smile. Now you've made it easier for them to be nicer. How does that feel instead?

> *Pay it forward and help them stay positive. Act with intention.*

What about your friends? You have less control over them. But did you really hope to hang out with them so that they could complain and have a bad time? Pay it forward and help them stay positive. Act with intention.

Now let's look at things the same way when it comes to eliminating self-complaint. This refers to the kind that's in your head and your inner monologue, even about the smallest things. What if, instead of being self-critical, you make a choice to coach and encourage yourself about how you'll do something better the next time?

When possible, give yourself the benefit of the doubt that you did nothing so terribly wrong in the first place. Maybe you're having a less than stellar day. That happens. Tomorrow is another day. Could this be a case of letting assumptive thinking cloud your self-perceptions?

Let's say there was something you said to your boss and, for whatever reason, believe that it came off the wrong way. You may be telling yourself, "I sounded like an idiot." However, instead of their somehow thinking less of you, that thing you said was well-received. In fact, your boss is thinking, "Wow, they really know their stuff!" Our perception filters and self-esteem play tricks on us all the time.

Then there's what you say to yourself and don't ever realize it, or not until after you've beaten yourself down. Stop. Just stop it.

Give yourself a break. How can you accurately assess your actions among the noise and negativity from your assumptions and continuous subconscious self-abuse?

Constructive self-criticism has its place. Who, besides us, will help us improve ourselves? If you're anything less than 100 percent certain you did anything wrong, what's the point of putting yourself down about it? This is akin to the logic of Earned Confidence and reminding yourself that there's no point in letting yourself worry about something not certain and that has yet to occur.

Life should be enjoyed not endured.

> **Life should be enjoyed not endured.**

There's a reasonably simple preventative measure and accessible remedy for all this complaining and self-abuse. In a word: Kindness.

Is negativity and stress ever worth it? That's a loaded question.

This comes back to self-sabotage. A lot of people deserve more than what they believe they can have and never get because they don't believe in themselves. What will it take to believe? What's standing in the way of seeing yourself as who you aspire to be?

Hold that thought. Before we end up down a rabbit hole of self-assessment, let's add some perspective about what we can and cannot control in our individual lives. There's a certain comfort in trying to control and make sense of whatever comes our way. In some cases, control is an illusion. In others, control is imposed upon us.

This brings us back to the belief some hold that "Things happen for a reason." My impression of that expression is that most people associate it with something unexplainable, which more often tends to be a positive event. Does it make sense to chalk things up to some sort of serendipity, shrug our shoulders and just go about our days? That's certainly the easy option.

As we approach the culmination of the book, I'd like to offer some food for thought to puts things into context. This clarification is self-contained, which is to say that it's entirely based on my own viewpoint as opposed to being sourced from external research.

Upon reflection, I believe that there are five causes for how things happen to us: randomly, unintentionally, intentionally, magnetically and/or because of what someone else does, which falls into the category of external influences. These are listed in the chart below. The title is a bit clunky but conveys the idea.

Causes of Occurrences (How Things Happen)		
Source Cause	**Positive/Neutral**	**Negative**
Random Unavoidable	Fortunate Happenstance	Unfortunate Tragic
Unintentional	Passively Unplanned Inadvertent	Preventable Unnecessary
Intentional	Incremental Achievement Effortful Inevitability [ones' *why*]	Self-defeating Self-destructive
Magnetic (Law of Attraction)	Mindful Gratefulness Optimistic Expectations	Unmindfully Arbitrary Pessimistic Expectations
External Influence	Purposeful Kindness Ripple Effect	Manipulation (Spiders) Ripple Effect

As you can see, each of the five causes are further segmented into positive and negative columns. Naturally, something completely random can happen either way as well as have a neutral impact. When we look at a cause being unintentional, it refers to something that was within our control or ability to prevent. However, the outcome either occurred in the absence of any action or as an alternative consequence. In other words, something unintentional in the negative column missed your dose of prevention.

Intentional causes are straightforward. On the positive side of our life experiences, we apply conscious thought, actions and willpower to accomplish something. It can be anything from simple, everyday tasks to fulfilling bigger goals through effortful achievement.

> *Optimism and pessimism tend to become self-fulfilling prophecies.*

Our in-depth exploration into the Law of Attraction covers how occurrences can be sourced magnetically. There's a cross-section here whereby positive outcomes result from intentionally Amplifying Gratitude versus an individual who experiences the unintentional, negative consequences of lacking mindfulness. I also want to reemphasize the influence of our expectations and how optimism and pessimism tend to become self-fulfilling prophecies.

As described, the final category involves events that are caused by others that may or may not be within our control to prevent or mitigate. When someone's actions affect us unintentionally, they cause a somewhat random ripple effect that can impact us positively or negatively.

However, more significant for our purposes is when others' actions are intentional and personally directed. On a positive note, here's where another person's kindness is directly beneficial.

An immediate example is that you're reading this book. Finally, there are negative consequences caused by the manipulative actions of Spidery individuals. We've given this topic its due.

Respectfully, I refrained from exploring any aspects of religious beliefs in a higher power as a source cause. These vary by individual interpretations. In any case, this Causes of Occurrences chart seems like a good topic for debate in our *Z-isms* Reader Forum. It would be awesome to hear what you think, especially for coming up with a better title!

Now that we've considered how things happen, it's time to answer some questions for ourselves.

It's safe to say that we've covered our share of topics, how they interrelate and how to apply them in everyday life. Now what? The obvious reason why there's no universal answer is that these questions refer to your life among others in it.

> ### *Come up with your Life Enrichment Action Plan and commit to taking that LEAP.*

One approach to Winning the Battle Within is to come up with your Life Enrichment Action Plan™ and commit to taking that LEAP. If there's any one theme that represents a common thread in the book, it's that personal development starts with commitment and progresses with practice. Think of it as a new sport or skill you want to master.

For your reference and consideration, below is a sample 90-day LEAP that encapsulates many of the key points made throughout the book. I hope you can put it to good use. You're worth it! The most sensible approach to get into action may be to buy yourself a journal or spiral notepad, which can help you stay accountable.

It's important to keep in mind that the remainder of this chapter is designed to recap the book by posing many questions that are designed to inspire self-reflection and help set priorities. The point is that what you're about to read all at once is meant to revisit and span 90 days or longer. Do your best not to be overwhelmed. You may want to grab a highlighter and your new journal to write down whatever parts and questions that resonate with you.

Setting goals that you consider achievable is still too vague and may even be a recipe for failure or setbacks. Instead, let's make this easier and do things in bite-sized chunks, which is to say they'll take very little time and a manageable amount of effort.

Take the first week to get your arms around everything. Each of these exercises should take 10 to 30 minutes. Make time. Then revisit later to more fully consider your priorities and how to pace yourself. If you're raring to go and want to plow through, go for it!

Day 1: Be Aware of Spiders

Think about the top 5 to 15 people currently in your life that you consider to be in your direct orbit. Now do a quick run-down by posing that yes or no question: Spider or non-Spider? Do they possess the character trait to selfishly manipulate others or do you know them to be too good-natured to do such a thing? How can you become and remain more aware among those Spiders to avoid their webs and protect yourself? If you know Aunt Jane, your boss or anyone decides to start pulling your strings, what conscious effort can you take to thwart them?

Day 2: Identify and Assess your Tribe

Who are the five closest people in your life? What does each Tribe member typically do to contribute or take away from your happiness? Do they tend to drain your energy or boost it? Among any you identify as energy vampires, to what degree can you better insulate yourself or reconsider whether they belong in your life?

You can't change the people around you, but you can change the people around you.

Who else instead of those individuals might belong in your inner circle and what actions could you take to deepen those relationships? There's a post I just saw that quotes an unknown source: "You can't change the people around you, but you can change the people around you." That's very clever!

Day 3: Determine your Dominant and Default Elements

Does this further clarify your self-identity? Is your dominant element the one you've always been or has your life experience shaped you to behave like a different element?

Now think of 5 to 15 family members, friends, coworkers or other people in your life. Start with your Tribe. You shouldn't have to overthink. Have fun with this exercise! Trust your gut. It's pretty cut and dry. How can you mitigate, neutralize or liberate yourself from individuals with whom you experience conflict, undue stress or consistent negativity?

If you must continue to interact with anyone with whom you tend to argue, can you instead make a conscious choice to diffuse those situations by knowing it's in your best interest to do so? In other words, can you douse that Fire by behaving as Water in the heat of that moment, even though it's not in your nature? If you cannot, why is that?

Day 4: Gratitude Exercise 1 – Take Inventory

Make a list of everything and anything for which you're grateful. Start with the basics – health, family, friends, life needs met – and work your way from material possessions to the weather outside. Consider some of the things you'd like to manifest in your life, be that relationships, financial abundance, more energy, freedom or other things that honor your values.

Day 5: Assess and Embrace your Earned Confidence

What life events have made you stronger? How can you apply this confidence to avoid worrying and at least be less anxious about things that haven't happened? Do you sweat the small stuff? If you doubt your ability to reduce worry and anxiety, why? How are those unnecessary emotions benefitting you and others you affect? That's a rhetorical question.

Are you holding onto past regrets that drain your life force? What will it take to forgive yourself once and for all? What negative thoughts and self-abuse might you recycle? If so, what specific things do you say to yourself? Do you experience conflict with others that may be based more on assumptions than facts?

To what degree do you let others judge you and how much do you care about appeasing them versus honoring yourself? Why does anyone else's opinion about you somehow matter more than your own? Does that make sense? What are the consequences of someone else's negative judgment if you were to go your own way?

As some might say "Haters gonna hate." How freeing will you find it to just stop worrying about what other people think and not letting that affect your emotional health and behavior?

> *Are you willing to deal with the consequences of being your true self?*

Are you willing to deal with the consequences of being your true self?

If the answer is no, then you'll benefit from asking that question again.

Day 6: Be Honest with Yourself and About Others

Ask yourself: how accurately do I perceive others and the world around me? Am I a good listener?

Are there people in my life with whom I've severed ties and might consider reconciliation? What would it mean to find and make peace?

Am I prone to self-sabotage and, if so, what is the source of that behavior? What harmful lifestyle habits do I have that would benefit me to stop doing? Do I lie and, if so, is it out of habit? What are my top 3 to 5 areas for self-improvement that would increase my quality of life? Don't worry about the difficulty, just list them.

This is also a good opportunity to evaluate yourself and others with the Mood Scale and be candid. Might I suffer from some sort of mood disorder? There's no shame in having imbalanced brain chemistry. Should I consult a professional? Am I resistant to taking medication that will help me feel better? If so, how can I overcome that self-stigma? Is there someone close to me who needs a true friend to help them get help? Am I that friend?

Day 7: Gratitude Exercise 2 / Self-Care Report Card

Do your first five minutes of focused thankfulness. Choose a time of day without distraction. You might do this first thing in the morning to help set the tone for the day or just before bedtime to take stock of what highlights helped make that day as good as it was. Lunchtime could be an ideal time to do a little bit of both.

I highly recommend you set a reminder to do this at the same time every day. If possible, just remain consistent, 11:11 might be an ideal time. Try to concentrate on just one thing at a time and stick with it. Focus and amplify your experience with gratitude to connect as deeply within yourself as possible. Expect the best.

Awesome job! Let's finish strong. In addition to at least five minutes of gratitude, take a few more to look over the Self-Care Report Card from Chapter 7, rate yourself for each of the four health activities and tally your score. How did you do? You can make this your personal accountability tool. It only takes a few minutes each week. Are you inspired to set some goals to do at least as well or better next week?

CONGRATULATIONS! Expecting that you've followed through, you have taken important steps to make meaningful progress to upgrade your life. Stay true to yourself. Let's keep the remainder of Month 1 at least as manageable as Week 1.

Now that we're going a week at a time, it's best to pace yourself with 20 to 30 minutes per day and set a deadline to achieve the following, likely by the end of day on Sundays. Decide the order for each day that will keep you moving forward and by how much. Be goal-driven and reward yourself for achievement.

Week 2: Reflection Exercises

It seems like a simple question to ask yourself, though may be anything but: *Who am I?*

With what do you associate your identity? Is that your career, your family life, your character traits, your aspirations? Take 10 minutes or 10 hours because it's probably been awhile since you've asked yourself this basic question. Then again, maybe this is something you've worked at your whole life. You might also consider doing a personality test, which are easy to find online. The next question, if not already clear, may be, "Who do I want to be?"

How do you feel about your self-worth? Do you truly love yourself? What can you do to improve that relationship? Are you too hard on yourself? If so, why is that? What will it take to be at peace with yourself and keep it? Can you find a special photo that you feel portrays your true self at your best? Frame it.

How would you describe your sense of adventure? What's still on your "Bucket List?"

> *Force yourself to stretch disbeliefs to view things optimistically.*

Do you tend to be an optimist or a pessimist? Try taking a Perception Snapshot every day this week. Go a step further. Choose 3 to 5 events this week that you could perceive with the opposite lens.

If you're more of a pessimist, here's where to force yourself to stretch disbeliefs to view things optimistically. If you're an optimist, take stock about how you see things favorably and *pretend* what it would be like to view the exact same circumstances in a negative light. The likely irony is that you'll experience even more gratitude knowing these aren't your true feelings.

> *What does it mean to you to become a better person?*

If you identify with being a Spider, are you willing to contain or curtail those manipulative behaviors? Leave your dark side in the past. How might doing so bolster your self-esteem and improve your life, such as by deepening relationships? What does it mean to you to become a better person? Are you willing to make amends with those you've harmed?

What can you do to be more in the moment?

What are 3 to 5 recent undesired events that you could have prevented with foresight and some contingency planning? After all, hindsight is 20/20. Take a good look.

What are some events that you think you handled deftly? Give yourself props!

What's causing you stress? Are there events and circumstances in your life that feel like you're swimming upstream or make you feel as if you're banging your head against a wall? What would it mean to turn around and swim with the current? Think about it while stretching for 10 minutes. Seriously, it's only 10 minutes.

What do you think of 11:11? Do you catch it? Do you find you're more in the flow when that happens? Practice the specific gratitude exercise in Chapter 11. You can do that in less than one minute.

What do you think of coincidences and being more proactive about making them matter? What have been some of the most unlikely coincidences in your life? Any thoughts about any meaning they may hold or what outcomes any yielded? Are there any loose ends worth revisiting and pursuing? Are you willing to track coincidences from now on and see where they lead? Have fun with it!

Revisit all your great progress from the first two weeks. Have another crack at your Self-Care Report Card and be proud of your healthy achievements. Begin to refine and formulate your Life Enrichment Action Plan for Month 2, especially based on what you've done to date and still want to try.

Week 3: Energy and Mood Management Self-Assessment

Assess your energy level and what you can do to improve it in your personal and professional life. If you were disciplined enough to improve health habits, what might that look like in your diet, exercise, consistent sleep, meditation, breaking or moderating destructive behaviors and/or improving life-work balance? Remember the 3-Day Rule. Make a pact with yourself to prevent a prolonged mood imbalance.

How would you rate your levels among the four core needs: physical energy, emotional connectedness, mental focus and spiritual alignment?

How can you trust your gut more?

Are you someone who gets caught up in analysis paralysis? How can you trust your gut more? Write it down.

How can you be more effective and efficient in your work life and maintain optimal energy and mental acuity? What would make you a better Life Athlete? Try doing productivity "sprints" to tackle your to do list. Try taking more frequent, brief breaks to move around and refocus. Monitor your energy and adapt as needed and able.

Consider going to bed earlier so you can get in the habit of waking up earlier. This could be especially helpful to replace the more stressful habit of a morning rush.

Revisit how you can reduce or eliminate conflict and other stressors that sap your energy and degrade your mood. How's progress with thwarting Spiders and strengthening your Tribe? Keep going.

Do something out of the ordinary. Step out of your comfort zone. It can be as simple as being outside and doing nothing but intently observing nature. Watch the trees blow. Play the cloud game. Do it for longer than you're comfortable. Then reflect on the experience. What was it like to be in the moment? What other ways can you have that experience on other days if only for a few minutes? What do you love enough to do even when no one else is watching? For what would you get uncomfortable?

Is there a reason you refuse to let go of what makes you sad?

Again, I'm posing a lot of questions here. They're not intended to be answered all at once. Focus on those that resonate and to which answers and actions will upgrade your life. P.S. It's also time for your third Report Card.

Week 4: Define Your *Why*, Pinpoint Inevitabilities, Set Goals as Milestones

What is your *why*? Is it powerful enough to fuel your energy, will, tenacity, grit, belief and faith in yourself to see it through? What does your passion fuel?

What are those Point B's? Cast your vision. Think through every detail you can.

Pinpoint your life Inevitability at Point B and draw a straight line back to yourself.

Achieving big goals are the cumulative result of incremental steps.

Now retrace that line moving forward. Rather than feel over-whelmed, what could be the next small steps? Write them down. Achieving big goals are the cumulative result of incremental steps. Determine the new habits that will help bring the above to fruition.

If there was any defining moment in your life to date, what would that be and why? And, if there were to be a redefining moment in your life to come, what would that be and why? This could range from major events – like marriage, kids, divorce or relocating – to your envisioning the results of making certain lifestyle changes.

An additional approach is to think back 2, 5 and 10 years ago. What's changed? What goals did you set then and to what degree have you brought them to fruition? How has your life improved and regressed? Now, let's revisit the vision you're casting for the next 2, 5 and 10 years.

What would you regret not doing or finishing what you started? How does it feel not to accomplish what you now aspire to do? In optimistic contrast, what's the best that can happen and how does that feel?

What remains absolutely necessary to happen in your life?

Just remember, complacency changes nothing. This is similar to knowing that it is better to have tried and failed than to have never tried at all. What momentum can you see yourself gaining?

Courage is contagious but first comes a fear to overcome.

What do you fear? What does it mean to step into your discomfort zone? What might you achieve there that would make you proud of yourself?

Sometimes the thing we want most is just one act of courage away.

> **Sometimes the thing we want most is just one act of courage away.**

It's alright for a lofty goal to be questionably achievable at most, but it still must be achievable. Put this in the context of Gladwell's *Outliers* and understand that achieving your biggest goals can rarely be done alone. As you envision that path of Inevitability, you may find glaring obstacles. What external resources and individuals will you need to overcome them and progress? Who else might you call upon to help and how? What passions do you share? Who do you need to meet? Who needs to meet you?

Here's where it's essential to be honest with yourself about what you know and what you know you can do. Also, contemplate what you think you know, what you think you don't know, what you know you don't know, and what you know you can't do.

There's also a factor of limited capacity. You are an energy source. You may well possess the mathematical equivalent of infinite willpower and unequivocal belief. You are undeterrable, but the inevitable outcome you aim to achieve will take more than that. Be realistic.

Bringing that ultimate goal to fruition may even exceed your lifespan, but it's still achievable by developing enough momentum and a succession plan to keep it going. The question then becomes what Inevitability will establish a reliable foundation to accomplish the bigger goal? We're bordering on business planning 201. Let's leave that for you to pursue.

Continue with your 5-minute daily gratitude exercise. Choose something different every day. This includes being grateful for having things you may not actually have yet. Remember your 5-minute perception challenge from Chapter 4? Consider trying that first. Pick a timely topic and transition into an exclusive focus on gratitude. How about taking another Perception Snapshot? Did I mention the Report Card? How have your grades trended these first four weeks?

Wow! You've completed Month 1! Whatever it is you were able to accomplish, be positive and proud. No matter how easy or difficult it seems, forming new habits and working toward making them a personal ritual involves self-challenge. This is also a good time to reflect. Consider revisiting your journal to gauge what went well and what went worse than expected.

You know better than anyone that you always get back up!

It's only human to encounter stagnation or experience a step backward now and again. Maybe you've taken a punch in the gut or been knocked down. You know better than anyone that you always get back up! Catch your breath. Draw upon your willpower to push forward beyond your setbacks. Decide whether you'll be better served by taking more baby steps. Be kind to yourself and take pride.

For every step backward, take two forward. Put another way, two steps forward and one back is still one step forward.

Month 2: Amplify Gratitude

I hope the detailed approach in Month 1 helps you establish a solid foundation to experience many different types of life upgrades. Here's where you're in the best position to customize your progression based on what resonates and matters most to you. What's important is for you to keep going and build momentum yet keep your efforts easily achievable and well-paced.

One suggestion is to habituate whatever you do, especially by dedicating the same time every day and make it a sacred commitment to enhance your life. Stay consistent with a focused approach. You'll likely find it beneficial to choose a single, overarching theme for your LEAP and to refine your goals.

One priority that rises above others is to concentrate on gratitude. In this case, build gratitude as you would a muscle each and every day, if only for a minute. Longer is better. Revisit the list you made in Week 1 and choose a select few for which you're already grateful.

Then select a few more things of what you want to manifest and imagine that you already have them.

Continue to enhance gratitude by integrating it into your daily routines. Force yourself to be more in the moment and mindful of your surroundings. Heighten your perceptions as you experience events and interactions with others. Enrich your conversations. Listen more intently. Force yourself to prevent letting your mind wander, especially about what you'll say next. Fight back any impulses to interrupt.

Enjoy the day. Acknowledge your feet touching the floor upon getting up every morning. Create rich, incredible experiences. Be mindful of your footsteps for 25 to 50 yards or so. How'd that go?

Rely on the gratitude techniques featured in Chapter 13, such as the 4-step exercise. It's all there for you to practice the Law of Attraction. No need to get head-deep in the parts about quantum physics. Simply adopt the scientific notion that all forms of matter and energy are attracted to that which is of like vibration. Just embrace it and be doubt-free. You have everything to gain. Amplify it even more by instilling gratitude into your belief system. Go all the way by embracing it with greater faith. Force yourself at first. Practice consistently, increasingly and intently.

> *Be very clear about what you desire. Focus on it singularly. Give it all your positive energy.*

Be very clear about what you desire. Focus on it singularly. Give it all your positive energy. Feel good! All you need to do is expect it. Imagine that you already have and experience it. Breathe intentionally. Be grateful.

Ideally, you'll continue to experiment with the one-minute gratitude exercise from Chapter 11 that you started doing in Week 2.

These practices are already embedded in conventional forms of meditation techniques, yoga and martial arts, like Tai Chi. Join a class. Enlist a friend to keep one another motivated and accountable. Keep going!

Over-complications and overthinking are not required. When was the last time you sat with your legs crossed and just closed your eyes and breathed mindfully to be at one with your thoughts? Has it been days, weeks, months, years or never?

All it takes is to compel yourself to observe whatever comes to mind and then focus on something you've chosen to think about with intention. For how long would you be willing, or have you ever tried to make more space in your days? Can you spare 2, 5, 10, 30 minutes?

How much simpler and easier can it be? Try it for one minute. Do it now or at your first opportunity. How'd that go? Would you be willing to practice this as part of your morning or evening routine? Will you work up to doing it longer, improve your focus and practice to increase your magnetism?

It doesn't sound like too much to make yourself do. Well, if you're committed enough to try, I'd be curious to know what you think of that experience. Maybe give it a go and see for how long you can stay consistent.

Lastly, if the example of experiencing a minimal amount of gratitude on a daily basis equates to going an inch deep and a mile wide, what would it be like to choose one day to go a mile deep by infusing it with gratitude every chance you get? Might something more intensive deepen your experience and appreciation? It's only one day. Can you come up with a good excuse not to do it? My thought exactly!

Just to reiterate, it's up to you to tailor your Life Enrichment Action Plan (LEAP.) Pinpoint the questions, exercises, activities and goals you want to improve. We just dedicated a full month to practice and amplify gratitude. It's simply a recommendation for how you can choose to go deep on something specific for a whole month. It also includes continuing with your other activities and relying on the weekly Report Card among whatever else you decide to customize your LEAP plan.

Month 3: One New Habit Per Week

As we continue our momentum in days 60 to 90 and beyond, we want to keep up with the habits we're already practicing, especially gratitude exercises.

Consider taking it a step further from Month 2. What if you were to try to experience a sense of Thanksgiving every Thursday, or another day for a month? Or, if you're content with the commitments you've already made, stay in that groove and try other things incrementally. How about hosting a dinner with family or friends for that simple reason?

For now, let's assume that you've stuck with whatever improvements you've made. However, it's still too early to assume that you've adopted the lifestyle habits you're working to develop. You may have heard that it takes approximately 21 days to form a new habit. However, in fact, that's highly unlikely.

> *Let's leave it to you to set goals and develop consistent habits.*

Actually, according to my informal Google search, the average is more like 66 days. That was based on only a 15-minute daily commitment. No one finds it easy. The ultimate question is how bad do you want a better life? Since you're already into personal development, let's leave it to you to set goals and develop consistent habits.

Knowing yourself, you might decide the third month will be a rinse and repeat of everything to date instead of biting off more than you can chew. Another option is to experiment with a few new exercises, such as doing one new habit every week. See what feels right, what's easy to reinforce and what you want to keep doing.

It's still vital to keep it small and manageable. Hold yourself accountable. If you haven't already, now would be when you'll want to set daily and/or weekly reminders on your phone.

All told, this is a sensible checkpoint where you can revisit and reset certain goals. A good place to start is to review your reflections in and since Week 1.

Here are some examples:

Maybe you're someone who is already into physical fitness and in decent shape, but it's even more necessary to manage stress better. Let's pinpoint and address that at the source to prevent those problems. You're in the habit of working out but now may be a good time to mix up your routine and reinvigorate that commitment.

Who in your life already lifts your spirits?

Revisit what relationships you've improved so far. Which ones and in what ways can you take more purposeful steps to enhance? Have you reconciled with anyone? If so, how's that going? Who in your life already lifts your spirits? Call and see them more often. Laugh more. Be in those moments and enrich those experiences.

Now that you've thought about those with whom you're closest, have you made any conscious decisions and taken actions to strengthen your Tribe? Reevaluate the sources of negativity and stress in your life. Remind yourself about Spiders and fiery individuals. What remaining stressors are still within your control to mitigate or eliminate? How's that mental armor holding up among all else?

Reflect about your experiences that have made you stronger. How have you applied that Earned Confidence in recent months? Can you think of situations where you did or may have found it beneficial? Are you worried and anxious about something right now? Put that situation and those feelings through your confidence filter and see how much you can alleviate that negativity and stress.

Be sure to take note of whether that concern was justified and, if so, how you handled that event in real-time. Had you worried and remained anxious, would that have served any positive purpose? That's another rhetorical question. Remind yourself and be proud of coping better and working at whatever pace is best for you.

Can you let those negative emotions roll off your shoulders instead?

Has a negative event occurred that, instead of calling your Tribe members to rehash all the details, you decided to spare everyone involved and yourself from experiencing them again? Can you let those negative emotions roll off your shoulders instead? Take pride in staying on track with your LEAP!

What circumstances do you have or have you had that make you feel like you're swimming against the current? What can/did you do to turn around and go with the flow? How did that go? Can this help you trust your gut more?

How's your energy level right now? Covering three months of potential life enrichment activities makes this chapter dense and intense. When might it be good to revisit it and get into action?

Have you made progress with confronting your past regrets? Only you can forgive yourself and live in the present tense without self-imposed burdens. How can you let go? Do you have a pattern of self-sabotage to overcome? What will it take to get out of your own way, cross finish lines and take pride in accomplishments?

Are you doing a better job of not making assumptions and giving others the benefit of any doubts instead? Are you able to see situations from multiple vantage points, even if you're not in agreement with others? How do you react when others make assumptions about you or when you feel judged negatively by someone whose opinion matters to you? Are they right? If you're not certain they are, then can you shrug it off and truly not internalize those judgments?

Have you ever tracked and evaluated your mood patterns? Making a habit out of doing your Perception Snapshot will help.

What kinds of things lift your spirits and prevent spirals? Have you reached out to someone close who may need your support?

> **How clear are you about defining your why?**

How clear are you about defining your *why*? How much do you want to earn a better life for yourself and your loved ones? What progress have you made since thinking this through in Week 4? Are you willing to put the work in to get to where you want to go and make it inevitable? If no, why not?

We've pondered quite a few questions. Answering the ultimate question involves deciding which ones you find worthwhile to act upon.

Are you ready to put some practical insights into action? Start by accepting that there are different ways to perceive the world, yourself and how to realize both to their fullest potential and greatest joy.

As much as life management and improvement techniques are consistent with conventional personal growth, the one variable unique to each of us is to define our purpose. Knowing your *why* not only fuels your motivation to take good care of yourself, it also shapes your life's destinations. Where do you want to be? What are you waiting for and why? In contrast, be your own parent and say no to everything that doesn't support your goals. Try not to isolate. If you are not located where your best day can be, then go there.

In the absence of change, nothing changes.

> **In the absence of change, nothing changes.**

Once again, between all the exercises and the many questions we just posed to help organize and focus your LEAP, it's natural to feel overwhelmed at first. It's not intended to be entirely prescriptive as much as it is to provide a variety of activities and exercises that you find worth pursuing.

Focus more on dedicating a certain amount of time in some consistent way that's feasible. Consider experimenting with 15-minute sprints. Set phone alerts. Don't overthink it. Trust your gut and keep it simple. Most of all, stay positive and be proud of striving to be your best self and enjoy life in moments.

Let's mix it up and get back to our final loose end from way, way back in Chapter 4 when we were talking about perception. What happened to the lonely, missing dollar? Did you think I'd forgotten? Has this question perplexed you ever since? What I like about this enigma is that it's quick to explain. What I love even more is that you can demonstrate it with actual currency, which makes it mysteriously convincing.

Here it is. There are two variables that change the math. One is adding the extra five $1.00 bills to the $30.00 the three travelers paid for the room. The other is that the room cost $25.00, not the $27.00 paid after their refund. Somewhere in the shuffle of those variables, *POOF!* That's the best explanation and I'm sticking to it. If you happen to consult a trustworthy mathematician and discover greater enlightenment, feel free to share your insights in the Reader Forum!

Now that we've almost found that dollar, it makes sense to wind down with some ways to simplify your Life Enrichment Action Plan. After all, you've just endured well over 100 questions embedded in 90 days of suggested structured activities.

Simplify your Life Enrichment Action Plan.

For whatever inspires you to take action, keep in mind that these are akin to learning to play a musical instrument, that you are your own life athlete and that your LEAP is unique to you. This means it's a work in progress. Take the opportunity to decide what kind of life you want for yourself and devote energy to your achievements.

To help make sense of it all, here's a condensed approach to plot your best next steps:

1. Gift yourself a journal or notebook and label it "My Z-isms," or something more to your liking.

2. Skim through this chapter and write down and prioritize only the things that resonate for you, especially about gratitude.

3. Commit to do everything in Week 1, then Week 2. Use your journal to capture the exercises and your progress. Give the Self-Care Report Card a try. You can do anything for two weeks or even less.

4. Either during or after those days, choose at least 3 activities you already do and integrate gratitude exercises. This can be while showering, doing the dishes, folding clothes, walking the dog or during downtime, such as when you are at a stoplight or traffic is at a standstill.

   The point of weaving this into your daily activities is that you won't need to commit more time to do them. It also leverages the power of association as a behavioral trigger to help you experience gratitude routinely.

5. Review your list and only choose the top 2 or 3 to go a mile deep. If feasible, designate a specific, consistent time of day to keep moving forward. Find or make 10 to 15 minutes to make yourself a priority. Set a daily alert on your phone and stick with it.

6. Reevaluate progress at the 30-day mark and recalibrate for the next 30 days to make it easily achievable.

7. If possible, be better to yourself than ever before. *Of course*, it's possible, so enjoy!

That completes the framework for those committed to achieving optimal life enrichment by taking the LEAP, so to speak.

Well, what if that's not you? What if you read *Z-isms* more out of curiosity and to gain some practical insights? Maybe you're already in a groove with personal development and are seeking ways to upgrade your routine. Maybe you simply need an emotional and motivational tune-up.

> *You simply need an emotional and motivational tune-up.*

On the flip side, maybe you consider yourself to be more of a "creature of habit," stuck in your ways, who is seeking more of an a la carte approach to improve your quality of life.

The answer has less to do with any judgment as it does my core desire for you to get the most benefit. Put another way, my goal is to make it impossible to come away from this book and not be better for it.

Even if your progress is incremental, aspire to keep moving forward by taking more steps than the number you ever feel knocked backward. You can persevere. It may take time to notice certain improvements. Be patient with and kind to yourself.

> *Be patient with and kind to yourself.*

Below is a shortlist that may be more of a Life Enrichment Menu than it is an Action Plan, which is to say these are about taking single steps rather than a LEAP.

For this purpose, thanks for understanding that the list is redundant to provide options to take specific actions today, tomorrow and/ or on any given day. You'll find these items offer ways to improve various aspects of self-awareness, relationships, mindfulness and enrichment overall.

- Rely on your Earned Confidence to defeat worry and anxiety

- Upgrade your Tribe, especially the five people closest to you

- Catch assumptions to prevent "phantom arguments"

- Avoid or mitigate conflict by agreeing which of you is the current

- Inventory what's preventable and take precautions

- Be open to differing perceptions, choose those most favorable and optimistic

- Keep taking your Perception Snapshots

- In conflict, remember that two "rights" don't make a wrong

- Choose reconciliation over retaliation

- Identify Spiders and avoid being ensnared

- Consider elemental traits and how they interact in your encounters

- Lift a finger instead of pointing one

- Treat others and their time with equal importance

- Be more energy-aware and mindfully manage yours

- Complete tasks based on energy rather than time consumption

- Consider life currencies and how to gain more freedom

- Practice doing "sprints" and taking intermittent breaks

- Heed the 3-Day Rule and treat yourself right to maintain mood balance

- Evaluate your work situation and potential actions for improvement

- Whenever the current shifts, adapt to swim in that direction

- Step outside of your comfort zone and expand it

- Visit StudentSTEPS.org and share the site with others in work transition

- Follow through on coincidences and experiment

- Try the one-minute gratitude gravity exercise

- Integrate gratitude into your daily life

- Believe in yourself, instead of being uncertain

- Be in the moment and make meaningful memories

- When there's no other way but through, remain poised

- Hold on tight until everything clears

- Forgive and free yourself of past regrets

- Focus on expectations; they tend to happen

- Win the Battle Within and allow self acceptance to fuel your personal growth and enjoyment

- Use the Self-Care Report Card (it only takes one minute)

- Join and participate in the Reader Forum (via Z-isms.com)

Any step forward is the right direction.

> *Believe in yourself, instead of being uncertain.*

We're almost there! If there's any final point to hit home, it's that *Z-isms* is actionable in that it promotes various life skills that involve a certain amount of consistent practice and thoughtfulness to make true progress and continuously improve. Set-backs, sluggishness and distractions are ordinary obstacles. These are worthy opponents to channel your inner Muhammad Ali and bring your trash talk to the boxing ring or, if you prefer, the ice rink!

Trust your Earned Confidence and *know* that you are extraordinary!

CHAPTER FIFTEEN

Walking the Talk

You may be done for the moment. Now it's my turn. If I'm going to dole out all this practical advice, then I feel compelled to follow through and walk the talk.

There's no time to waste. Here we go. It's my **Day 1**. Writing this final chapter coincides with starting a new journal and calling it "My Z-isms," along with going through the first two weeks of exercises.

It's time for me to do other things for a while.

BOOM! I'm back. It's **Day 15**. Wow, those two weeks really flew by! Here are some highlights of my personal LEAP activities:

Z-isms Exercises: Although I'm very familiar with the likes of Spiders, my Tribe and my elemental traits, I still did the exercises and logged them in the first pages of my journal. There weren't many surprises among those closest to me, though I did enjoy assessing some newer people in my life who I had yet to consider in these ways. As mentioned previously, we live in a new neighborhood. So that kept me busy.

Another realization is that I've been out of touch with my circle of friends and that I'd like to reconnect and be more social. I've let the book consume me a bit. We also have a few neighbors we've talked about having over and think it's time to make plans. I also owe my big brother and sister a call. Clearly, the highest priority is to have extra date nights!

Workout/Weight Loss: I admit to overdoing it this year. I also fell out of being consistent with an exercise routine. Putting on weight has made my cardio fitness noticeably worse. Let's just say that playing hockey with the equivalent of two 10-pound dumbbells strapped to my waist hasn't improved my game.

I was off to a good start the first week with some form of physical exercise for at least 20-minutes every day, except one. This involved either playing hockey, lifting, stretching or getting the cobwebs off the Peloton. Thank you Ibuprofen! I scored an easy A on my first Self-Care Report Card and squeaked by with another in Week 2.

The tail wagged the dog, as the saying goes.

I confess to slacking a couple of times the second week. One of those days was when something unexpected happened. The tail wagged the dog, as the saying goes. That's life. It also seemed harder to get back on track then at first, which I didn't expect. I had to push through some quicksand, but afterward, I was glad I did.

On a positive note, I also started a new 30-day system with Isagenix, which is also important to me in Walking the Talk. I've lost 9 pounds already!

Gratitude/Mindfulness: I blocked out 15 minutes the past two Tuesdays, Thursdays and Saturdays to focus on the Law of Attraction. I made a conscious decision to connect with gratitude upon waking up and my feet touching the floor. This continued with me being more mindful during my morning routine, during downtime, sitting at stoplights and while doing household tasks.

> *Being mindful has noticeably helped me feel more in the flow.*

I also caught 11:11 a bunch of times and did the 1-minute gravity exercise, including one at the rink. I've been less consistent with that habit lately and it was nice to reconnect and do it full-on. Being mindful has noticeably helped me feel more in the flow.

Daily Routine Chart: This was a one-time thing, but I decided to inventory how I spend my time, especially for self-care. I used the first page of my new journal to chart my current daily habits. The task was to capture every detail, no matter how small. I separated them by morning, day and night – everything from showering and feeding the cats to preparing meals and taking my supplements.

Then I added a few things that were easy to incorporate. That included the gratitude exercises mentioned above and making sure to drink at least one bottle of water in each part of the day. Erica always has her water bottle close by, so it was easy to remember to do myself. I made a few notes about routine activities that are closer to weekly, like doing laundry, taking out the trash, changing the litter and yard work.

The idea was to assign some behavioral triggers that make it easier to associate new habits with existing ones.

It seemed a bit extreme to list all the mundane details but I was glad to have the snapshot to create some structure for my self-improvement project.

I also designated 11 a.m. for 20 minutes of something, depending on how I was feeling. That block of time could include exercising, meditating or stretching. Whenever that time had a conflict, I made myself do the above at the beginning of the next available hour or earlier. This has allowed me to wake up, do a "work sprint" to get whatever off my plate and recharge while doing those physical activities.

That's all I decided to take on in these early weeks. Plus, I want to keep the momentum going. That's my report so far.

And we're back! Yes, it's now **Day 30**. Here's my update: I scored a solid B on these last two Report Cards, which is self-respectable.

Workout/Weight Loss: I didn't quite hit my goal, which is to say I was still less consistent with the daily workouts. However, I did manage to make myself do it five times each week. I'm also still paying the price for not using the Peloton for so long. Did I mention Ibuprofen?

I've stayed on track with my weight improvement plan. I'm stoked to share that I'm now down 14.5 pounds, which leaves 5.5 pounds until I hit my goal weight! I feel so much better and have more energy, which also helps my motivation to workout. I've noticed that my mood is more consistently upbeat. My mental acuity and stamina are also markedly improved. I think it's mostly due to the weight loss as well as having less to digest during the day.

Perception Snapshot: The tool in the book is super easy and takes just about no time flat. Knowing that I tend to view things in a positive light, most of my life priorities had plus signs. There are at least two that would be at least as easy for me to put in the other column. Seeing things on the bright side and summoning some added hopefulness is a big help. I also found this exercise helped me sharpen my focus on gratitude.

The one item that didn't make it to the plus column is work/life balance. I've often heard myself say that being an entrepreneur means that my business and personal lives are one in the same, which simply isn't true. It's easy to fall into the trap of having that mentality. I've definitely allowed myself to be fun-deprived for much longer than I'd realized. While the book will continue to consume me for a while, it's definitely time to plan and look forward to doing something special.

Gratitude/Meditation: For the most part, I've stayed consistent with practicing mindfulness, be that in catching 11:11 most days and Amplifying Gratitude at stop lights and so forth. I don't do it at every one, just here and there.

RESULTS MAY EXCEED EXPECTATIONS

I've also tried to step it up by trying out meditation techniques for 10 minutes every other day. This has mainly focused on intentional breathing exercises, which I really like. At first, it was much harder to meditate than expected. I found it awkward, especially with the silence. I also kept checking the clock. My mind wandered a lot. It still does, but not as much. I'm getting better at bringing myself back into focus.

Of course, breathing is at the source of meditation and the key to awareness to access one's higher self. Can you tell I'm not the first person to say that?

> **Breathing is at the source of meditation and the key to awareness to access one's higher self.**

I was starting to feel a sense that I wouldn't stick with it but I decided I'm not letting myself have an excuse to stop. I made some adjustments by switching to a chair, using a sound machine and setting a timer. These helped but they still weren't enough.

This led to doing what I should have done in the first place, which is downloading an app for mindful meditation and letting that be my guide. It's only been this past week that I've used it but it has made a huge difference. I am calmer and less stressed, which I didn't realize I had been feeling until "releasing" it.

It's going to take a lot more practice to fully harness my inner Zen!

One other key point is that I'm using a calendar alert to make this more like a ritual than a routine. I know myself and, without that structure, even those 10 minutes wouldn't happen.

Vision Board: This is still a work in progress. I spent about 45 minutes to visualize new goals with the main one having the book be a success and opening certain doors to even greater opportunities. It's a start.

Sleep Schedule: I'm a little more of a Night Owl than for my own good. I know it would be better to wake up earlier. I thought about shifting my schedule by an hour but I figured that might be too much all at once. Instead I went with 30 minutes, which has been easy. Even that little extra time in the morning has helped me feel more mindful and productive. At some point, this will help encourage me to shift another 30 minutes but I'm not ready to commit to that yet.

I also think it might be better to switch my 10-minute gratitude meditation into this slot and have that be part of my daily ritual.

News Diet: One other decision to help me stay on track was to identify a "time drain" that I could do without or cut back in these early stages. For me, it's been watching too much news. Yes, I'm officially on a "News Diet!" That means no TV pundits, but I do allow myself to use my phone to see what's going on.

It has turned out to be more than a time-saver. It's also reduced some negative energy about what's going on and has spared me the residual impact of having those thoughts involuntarily stressing my brain. I didn't realize how much that negativity affected me mentally and emotionally until I felt that sense of relief.

These are not huge sacrifices to make in exchange for improving my well-being and upgrading my life.

I've actually gained time beyond what I've committed to my personal LEAP. I'll also free up more time in the coming weeks by not getting into another show to binge watch to replace the one Erica and I are about to finish. There's also a game on my phone that I could play less or give up entirely, though I do still have my "mindless" time to fill. These are not huge sacrifices to make in exchange for improving my well-being and upgrading my life.

All these activities in these first 30 days might seem like a no-brainer and very easy, but that's only on paper. Even though they're only incremental changes, it's taken a lot of discipline to do what's easier said than done. I also think it will be better to move the 11 a.m. time slot to earlier and make it part of an extended morning routine. Either way, I know that having a dedicated time is my key to stay consistent and keep going.

Others might have different approaches, but this is the one that works for me to keep my commitment to myself and make it much more manageable.

This month has also helped me build confidence about Walking the Talk and knowing that I'll maintain and build more momentum. The operative clichés I'm telling myself to be accountable are, "You can do anything for 30 days," and the ever-predictable, "Just Do It!"

Overall, I'm genuinely proud of myself for following through and having significant results to share, especially with the weight loss.

Looking over my Life Enrichment Action Plan, I can and will do more to amplify gratitude this coming month and beyond, though am definitely not ready for a bigger commitment like yoga or Tai Chi. Maybe I'll search for some options on YouTube and in the Peloton video library. I didn't realize it also has stretching and guided meditation sessions.

It's too soon to decide and commit to whatever new habits I'll take on in Month 3, and it may only be one or two instead of something new every week. It will depend on the size of the commitments that are involved. I'll know soon enough.

My original plan for this chapter was to track and share it for 30 days, however, today is now **Day 58**.

I'm running out of runway and need to decide to declare the book done. I've been focused on the editing stage but I feel compelled to extend the book one last time. Although in its final edit, I've had to make an unexpected adjustment.

In the spirit of full disclosure, my LEAP started veering about 2 weeks ago and it's been challenging to get back on track. I've decided it's necessary to self-prescribe more structure by making myself rotate priorities by doing things in one-hour time blocks.

I've started with a minimum of 6 hours on weekdays and 3 hours on weekends, which is too manageable to let myself off the hook. This involves doing work sprints by using my phone alarm like an egg timer because I like the added sense of urgency. Erica is actually better at this and she's been more of an "accountability partner," which could be a good idea for you to consider enlisting.

I now must be up by 7 a.m. and do my morning routine by 8 a.m. I rotate my work day around 3 priorities: The Internship Institute, Isagenix and the book for which I need to turn my attention to marketing. Whenever I have calls or meetings, those hours are spoken for. Otherwise I can choose to do whichever whenever, but I try to put in at least an hour per day for each one. The book has tipped the scales.

I've also decided to build in either a full hour or two 30-minute slots for "me time," which is mainly for stretching, exercising and/or meditation and gratitude exercises. Three days per week must be for cardio, which is essential for my mood health. This doesn't include playing hockey, which I do at least twice a week. This will keep me consistent with my Report Card too.

I also have to spend about 10 to 15 minutes each night to reflect on my progress and complete by making journal entries. If I somehow go to bed without doing it, then I must do it first thing. That commitment has been the hardest to keep but I'm sticking with it. Lastly, I frame out my priorities for the next day to start it with focus and purpose.

> *There's nothing quite like not giving yourself a choice to do something.*

There's nothing quite like not giving yourself a choice to do something to make you do something!

I'd be less than forthcoming if I said

it's been easy these past few days. On the flip side, it's been working very well. The egg timer idea keeps me focused and productive. I've been crushing it! In addition, I did hit my goal weight last week and have kept it off. I'm incredibly happy and proud about that!

Knowing myself, I recognize that creating this much structure isn't sustainable. Too many things unexpectedly demand my attention on any given day. However, going overboard for another week or two will force me into a better groove and still give me a lot of progress to show for it. Plus, I'll feel good about putting myself through the paces.

With that, it's time to call it a day, at least for my LEAP routine.

In closing, one loose end I'd like to tie is with the title. With my sincerest respect for non-American readers and the 26th letter of our alphabet, I'd like to set the record straight about the pronunciation being "Zee," not "Zed." However, just in case you "Zed-isms" enthusiasts would like a refresher:

Z-ism [Zee-iz-*u*m] (Noun)

Pearls of wisdom, original wit or personal experience shared to positively impact as many people as possible; Insights to Live By.

More specifically, if you were asked right now to share one of your "go-to" catch phrases, what might that be? It could be something that a relative passed down as a legacy for you to impart to your kids and others. Is it original? Maybe you adopted it from an unknown source. Might there be a story behind it? What do you regard as life lessons learned?

Those are *your* Z-isms.

Epilogue

Arriving at the end of the book is just the beginning.

Whether you decide to go all-out and follow your LEAP, adopt certain practices like the Self-Care Report Card, or simply come away with more *Insights to Live By*, I sincerely hope you found *Z-isms* well worth the read and that it makes a meaningful difference to enrich your life as well as has a contagious effect among those around you.

With that in mind, please consider paying it forward and recommending the book to those you think will benefit. Aside from *Z-isms* being about what I wish my younger self would have known, I'd like to think it covers much of what just about anyone needs to know to improve and enrich their lives.

I greatly appreciate your helping me to achieve my *why* in that way. It also would be all-the-more meaningful for the book to ultimately help fund the nonprofit to allow me see through that part of my life's work.

For me, the nonprofit is about creating opportunities with exponential potential to help people get on the right path and earn a good living. The book is about cultivating personal success and the exponential potential of a like-minded community by encouraging shared growth and the value of freedom.

It's time to find that new Point B and line up some more dominos! I think I'll have a beer first. Make that at least two!

What now?

That sounds like a better question for you.

As mentioned, you are cordially invited to join the Reader Forum, a private group exclusively for you and others with a commitment to life enrichment to continue to interact together and with me.

My goal is to foster an ever-expanding, close-knit community of difference-makers and mindful individuals who share their thoughts and experiences that they think would benefit others to know.

The Reader Forum allows anyone and everyone to promote their Z-isms and meaningful experiences in service to a greater good. It would be amazing to have your unique wisdom further empower others and create value beyond the book.

Another dimension of this group is its level of intimacy that will allow me to forge a greater trust with readers and elaborate about various topics. Battling billionaires and earning some of Bill Gates' money aside, there's only so much I could include in *Z-isms*. I welcome the opportunity to interact, field questions and delve into other topics that didn't find their way into the book.

 Whatever your takeaways, I genuinely hope you found an abundance of *Insights to Live By* to make what's important to you that much better. I know you can do it and so do you! You've already shown up.

Infinite possibilities are ahead!

What you expect, tends to happen.

Wishing you the very best for an enriched, purposeful, healthy, long, prosperous and fulfilling life!

P.S. In honor of your commitment to life enrichment, the secret phrase to join the private Reader Forum is "Take the LEAP." This group is accessible via Z-isms.com.

The photos that appear throughout the book are among my favorites. Naturally, there was only so much I could say about each one in the main text. In case you're curious, I'm happy to share more details.

Our Engagement:
The date was 4/22/17, I took Erica to New York City for the weekend for what she thought was to celebrate her birthday. My plan was to propose in a rowboat there in Central Park but the weather had other ideas. I soon learned that rowboats don't row in the rain. My spontaneous Plan B worked out even better. We walked to the iconic Bethesda Fountain and Terrace where my hidden photographer could get the best shot.

The Barefoot Pyramid:
It was early in the summer of 1982 on Eagle Lake in Northern Ontario where I was fortunate to be at the hockey camp there. Two of the top waterski instructors had the idea and asked me to attempt this feat with them. Back then, this had only been achieved a handful of times. The photo was published along with a full article in the August issue of *Ski Nautique News*, the official publication of the Canadian Waterski Association.

My Hockey Stance (02.20):
As we got onto the ice for warm-ups before a game, I said to Frank, "Yo Frank, do me a favor. Go stand in net and look like a goalie." He came through! I also enjoyed a special occasion to bring my Temple captain's jersey out of retirement.

Fun Fact: The photo in Chapter One of the book was cropped a bit more. As you can see here, we realized after the fact that the rink clock read 3:33.

Coincidence?

Our Bengal Refuge: It's no coincidence that Zoey is in front. She's always the center of attention. On the chair to the left is her sister Paizley. She's the lap cat in the family. They just had their first birthday. Last, but not least, is Buzz. He's very laid back and set in his ways. They're all rescues and get along really well. Did you notice that their names all have Z's?

My Fam (06.19): Since Greta and Jake are mentioned numerous times and Erica is hidden by her hand and umbrella in Central Park, I'm grateful to be able to share this photo of us together. This was taken at a rehearsal dinner for my nephew's wedding.

Secret Post-Script

We *all* deserve to have more fun and joy in our lives.

In this moment, it's to welcome you to the Secret Post-Script and invite you in.

That's right, as NOT seen in the *Z-isms* Table of Contents is this spontaneous hidden chapter. Just when you thought my last addition was after Making Coincidences Matter and that call with my brother and sister, here we are.

The difference here is that we're winging it by writing a chapter in under 24 hours and publishing the final print version without the benefit of having a second pair of eyes. We're flying without a safety net here people! What would you like to do about how this book actually ends? Any requests?

Well, if I were to break it down, it has a combination of two parts Walking the Talk; two parts Amplifying Gratitude; one part as an entry into *My Z-isms* personal journal; and, two parts bringing this Inevitability to fruition. How many parts is that anyway? One of us may have lost count.

Let's calibrate our compass here. While it's time to call it a day, the good news is that I hit my mark! The *Z-isms* eBook will be up for sale on LEAP Day! I'm sure you don't need to guess how my deadline came about.

> **I'm not sure there's anything left of me to put in the book.**

We'll need these few days to make the rest happen. I guess my going for it here makes it an official fact that I can't say I didn't give it my all until the very end. I've left nothing on the table. I'm not sure there's anything left of me to put in the book. I guess we'll find out soon enough with the Forum being live!

Can you tell how epically stoked I am! It's almost surreal to know that we're going to press! By this time next week, I'll be holding the first paperback of *Z-isms* in my hands and will make sure it's ready for prime time!

It took a while but I finally feel really good about the book. As hard as I've tried to keep it clean in multiple ways, I know I'm imperfect enough to expect some mistakes, especially with so many late additions.

I'm just not going to sweat it and trust that you'll look past a typo or two and give me a break on at least one dangling participle. Whatever the book ends up being, it feels good enough for me, so I'm happy about having cool readers!

If any one thing is for sure, it's that this is also the one and only edition of *Z-isms* and my one and only personal development and enrichment book. The main reason is that we're taking our conversation offline, which is to say online in our exclusive and free Reader Forum.

I'm looking forward to staying engaged and getting better acquainted for as long as anyone wants to hang out with me. Come to think of it, I'm alright with going stag and keeping myself entertained.

Though I've been thinking about this book for at least fifteen years, it's been just under 9 months to get it to this actual point. Given that time and effort, the natural comparison may be to giving birth.

That thought sparks some parting words of advice to my fellow members of the male species. Never, no matter what, compare anything you ever do to childbirth. Play it safe!

As challenging as it's all been to date, I'm about to start a new job as a book marketer. The nice part is that the experience from my first career will be helpful, but only up to a certain point. Even still, this is the steepest learning curve I've ever faced. It makes writing the book seem like the easy part.

Just when I expected to feel done, I suddenly realize that *Z-isms* is only the beginning of this new life chapter. Stepping even more out of my comfort zone includes embracing this defined paradigm shift of my *why*, my self-identity and my expectations in life.

Most importantly is that I have one less major goal that I won't regret not achieving.

I feel an even greater sense of purpose to get to work and make even more progress. It's more than just about the book and it being a clean slate. It's an opportunity to apply my passion while swimming *with* the current instead of nearly drowning in the tide of internships.

For as long and as hard as I've had to kick and claw my way through pioneering the internship frontier, it's been beyond obvious lately how I've never felt the current flow so fiercely against me.

Sometimes the best decision is knowing when to quit.

In deciding to take a sabbatical from the nonprofit, I feel less conflicted about it being the right thing to do. You'll also recall my limitations with having "man brain." I'm only capable of doing one thing well at a time. If I tried to split my attention in marketing the book, both would fail. Sometimes, as hard as we ever try, the best decision is knowing when to quit or at least take a break.

In any case, I'm excited to take on new challenges and do what it takes to learn on the job. This is my new Point A. I am also well-aware of the fact that very few authors gain traction. I believe it's something like less than 1% of books sell more than 50,000 copies.

In fact, the vast majority of authors sell less than 100 books as well as that many thousands of similar books are published every day. At the time I found this out, I decided to write something on my whiteboard that's been within two feet of my view: "Defy the Odds."

The major difference in those dramatic numbers is that the motive beyond publishing for most nonprofit authors has less to do with selling books. It's more likely that they're professionals who want to increase their credibility for business development purposes and/or seek to position themselves for speaking or media appearances. Then there are those with money to burn and an ego to stroke.

One thing most of these authors have in common is the ability to write it off as a business expense. For my part, *Z-isms* has been funded out of my own pocket. I had to form my own publishing company. Unfortunately, it still didn't see fit to offer me a multimillion dollar advance or any distribution support. We'll show them a thing or two! Wait, that's me!

I couldn't hire publicists or writers or invest in anything like some authors who are willing to take a loss. It's also not written with those ulterior motives. It's written to – can you guess – positively impact as many people as possible. I'm pretty sure you got that one right.

Above all, I believe in myself, the *Z-isms* body of work and expect to defy all odds. There's hope for me yet! Have you heard the one about how the vast majority of financially successful people either played a sport, served in the military or trained in the martial arts? Can you believe that? It sounds true to me, at least in terms of it being a majority. The rest comes down to purpose and grit.

To me, this book was too important not to write. For one, Zman had to be brought to life for his inevitable destiny to come to fruition. Did you not realize that this has all been for Zman this whole time?. It's an understatement to say that it's close to my heart. You've heard and know more than enough of the rest.

This all points back and falls in the realm of Inevitability. Naturally, my Point A today is about putting the last touches on the book and returning to my days as a marketer.

If we take the long view to see as far as possible to our Point B, then I suppose the utmost, Utopian Inevitability for *Z-isms* is to be read by every English-literate human being on our planet, at least in terms of preceding any audio book or publishing translated editions.

In closer proximity and a more realistic view is to embrace the belief, expectation and experience of stepping into the roll of someone who knows fewer people than the number of those who know me.

All of this is well and good, but what matters is a realistic view and approach from the vantage point of practicality. These priorities are to envision the key happenings, contingencies and obstacles to circumvent and navigate the straightest way through. Thankfully, I can turn to some trusted professionals, great friends and family to have my back. This brings us back to Gladwell's *Outliers* and how one cannot achieve lofty goals alone. The book is no different.

One cannot achieve lofty goals alone.

It also intersects with Gladwell's work with *The Tipping Point* about how to turn a book like *Z-isms* into something trend-worthy. You may know that the answer is based on interacting with and catching the attention of "Connectors" and "Mavens" who will drive book recommendations by word-of-mouth.

As I further define my current Point B within sight, a lot of it involves straightforward tactical planning and goal-setting. It all culminates with framing certain expectations to manifest my Inevitability.

Any one of any number of dominos may be that tipping point. It's literally created from our own resourcefulness, ingenuity and sheer will. It's effortful. What I can guarantee is that I'm about to give it my best shot.

Are we toppling pre-tipping point dominos here? Another major factor in the tactical scheme is a function of creativity and professional experience from my first career. In a sense, my new job with the book brings me full circle to my marketing days. In fact, the Zcommunication.com site is now a favorite antique site (circa 2002), which is to say every word remains untouched by time.

When I ask myself if there's any one sentence I'd want my readers to come away with saying about the book, it's something like,

"If you LIKE *The Secret*, you'll **LOVE** *Z-isms!*"

As surreal as it may currently seem to describe this in the same breath as that exceptional body of work, Rhonda Byrne would be the first to say that that's necessary to believe, especially because most good books gain momentum by word-of-mouth. This goes to the very heart of that first career of mine and my focus on being a communication management and marketing strategist.

By associating *Z-isms* with an amazing legacy like *The Secret*, its reputation and loyal readership is at least the same. In addition to "piggybacking" off that halo and reaching many of my future readers, it's also a "triggering" strategy. The best example of this is the campaign many years back by the National Fire Safety Council about how we need to change our smoke detector batteries whenever we turn our clocks back and ahead. Brilliant! Few initiatives have stood the test of time and in such a powerful and impactful way. I've missed my first career!

So if you *happen* to want to mention our book to anyone else, I surely encourage and appreciate your saying something like,

"If you LIKE *The Secret*, you'll **LOVE** *Z-isms!*"

Could including this suggestion in the book be all it needs to fulfill its Inevitability? A more concrete example is among some of that exciting news I got this week.

I am bartering with a book publicist who sets up radio and podcast interviews and is going to secure 20 placements in high-profile media! I'm also providing some value in return and would like to think that my side of our two-way street is at least as wide.

Does this other news confirm that, it alone, could be all it takes to tip the rest of the dominos? Am I already on the other side of my tipping point? Has our Inevitability with *Z-isms* already occurred, except in the future? Cue the background music and sound effects!

> **Has our Inevitability with Z-isms already occurred, except in the future?**

Let's take one other quick snapshot of how this is working by fast-forwarding closer to some dominos in action. In this case, it's that I envision doing speaking engagements to promote the book and motivate people. In thinking that through, there have been times that I've imagined myself being on a large stage. When I was a kid, my dad thought I'd make a good stand-up comic. Umm, that's a hard pass! One open-mic night was enough to check that box.

Let's get clearer about this expectation. There's a large, enthusiastic audience with whom I share stories from the book, among others. My goal is to inspire and motivate. We are laughing together. The feeling is amazing!

There are some personal experiences that provide moving moments. Then there is rousing applause, of course! I especially enjoy staying after to personalize books for as many people as are interested to meet. Hold that thought!

> **I look around and see how Erica has made us the most beautiful home.**

Naturally, it's at least as essential to manifest Inevitability by experiencing this shift in my personal life. For example, I look around and see how Erica has made us the most beautiful home. No acknowledgement can do her justice. My one true love couldn't have been more supportive while I've been writing the book. I am beginning to see how this is where a deserving author belongs. I especially look forward to our plans to celebrate tonight.

There's one final aspect I'd like to share about the furthermost Point B of my current *why*. In other words, if I squint really hard and then harder, it's the domino I can still see. This is well beyond bringing the nonprofit to fruition. Once we reach that tipping point with the organization becoming financially self-sustainable, we'll repurpose some of the proceeds from the book and related endeavors to provide seed capital for worthy nonprofits that, like The Internship Institute, have been unable to fund and sustain themselves without seed capital.

Well, with my background in journalism, I've always been a fan of saying that there's nothing quite like a deadline to make something happen and I'm literally out of time.

I'd say the one major plan this deadline foiled is that I've been having a hard time letting all the blank pages in the back of many chapters go to waste. It's kind of the same thing as my mom insisting I clear all the food off my plate. On the other hand, I now choose these pages to be a welcome opportunity to give my readers a break.

It looks like all that content I had in mind will have to wait! I just might have a few more things left to say. Did I mention that there's a free, exclusive private Reader Forum to which you're cordially invited? Bring *your* Z-isms and let's keep it going!

In case you hadn't noticed, saying goodbye is not my strong suit. Sooo, I'll just leave you with this for now:

There's another disclosure about this Secret Post-Script that I've been holding back. The real purpose of this chapter is not to divulge a personal entry from my journal, it's been to share a "Celebratory Toast."

You read that right. I wrote it for us to hang out just a little while longer and have a beer together in a tall, frosty glass. But it seems the only difference is that one of us has gotten a solid head start!

CHEERS ALL!

#BeTheDifference

Acknowledgements

To Erica, my one true love, for all your support, encouragement and inspiration. I love you more and more every day!

To Jake, for all you've taught and inspired me. I could not be prouder of you and the fact that I get to be your dad. You also make an excellent editor!

To Greta, the brightest of lights, for your daily doses of humility that remind me how uncool I am. You and your mad skills never cease to amaze me!

To my big brother, Mark, and my sister Andrea, for being there when I needed you most.

To "mah brah," Mike, for your technical prowess and moral support and especially for all our color commentary about our Philadelphia Flyers!

Thank you also to Kathy, Jim and Erik Coover, along with our entire Isagenix team, for your vision, dedication and ingenuity that grant us the freedom we enjoy.

I am grateful for the opportunity to work with Nancy Lee Schnabel on the book cover and interior design along with our numerous collaborations in recent years and in those to come.

Special thanks to Martha Bullen of Bullen Publishing Services, Scott Lorenz of Westwind Communications and Heather Huzovic, media expert and Deana Riddle of BookStarter for bringing *Z-isms* to life and making it accessible to positively impact more readers.

Eternal appreciation continues for the hundreds of interns with whom I've had the privilege to team up, especially more recently: Craig J, Jacob C., Lindsey H., Sarah F., Alyssa M. and Megan B. Thanks for all your great work together and with the book launch!

Works Cited

Chapter 1

Pearl Jam. Song lyric from *Present Tense*. Album: *No Code*, 1996

Chapter 4

Antinori, Anna, L. Carter, L.D. Smillie, Seeing it both way: Openness to experience and binocular rivalry suppression, *Journal of Research in Personality*, Volume 68, June 2017

Merriam-Webster, Incorporated. definition: Perception.

Merriam-Webster, Incorporated. definition: Objectivity.

Chapter 5

The Mayo Clinic, *clinical descriptions of depression, mania, and hypomania.* Rochester, MN: 1889

Chapter 6

Gladwell, Malcom. *Blink.*
New York: Little Brown and Company, 2005

Chapter 7

Burchard, Brendon, *High Performance Habits.*
New York: Hay House, 2017

Loehr, Jim, and Tony Schwartz. *The Power of Full Engagement.*
New York: The Free Press, 2005

Chapter 8

Esalen Institute. Mind-Body Movement Connection Course, Big Sur, CA: 1993

Chapter 9

Gladwell, Malcom. *Blink*. IBID

Chapter 10

Merriam-Webster, Incorporated. definition: Coincidences. IBID

Chapter 12

Byrne, Rhonda. *The Secret*. New York: Atria Books, 2006

Ray, James Arthur. Quotation. *The Secret*, IBID.
www.jamesray.com

Chapter 13

Gladwell, Malcom. *The Tipping Point*.
New York: Little Brown and Company, 2000

Gladwell, Malcom. *Outliers*. New York: Little Brown and
Company, 2008

Jessica Schmitt Photography. *Engagement Photo*.
New York Central Park, 4.22.16

The Pursuit of Happyness. Columbia Pictures, 2006

Secret Post Script

Byrne, Rhonda. *The Secret*. New York: Atria Books, 2006

Gladwell, Malcom. *The Tipping Point*.
New York: Little Brown and Company, 2000

Gladwell, Malcom. *Outliers*. New York: Little Brown and
Company, 2008

About the Author

Matt Zinman is a difference-maker devoted to personally enrich the lives of at least 100 million people by 2025. His book, Z-isms: Insights to Live By, is based on his varied experiences as an entrepreneur, athlete, single parent, caregiver, consultant and nonprofit founder. Matt is also the host of "Insights to Live By," a podcast that invites guests to share their own pearls of wisdom.

In addition to his earned insights about self-discovery, relationships, amplified awareness and life enrichment, , Matt is CEO of The Internship Institute, which he established in 2007 to bridge the gap between education and employment while cultivating opportunity for students, veterans, businesses, nonprofits and communities. The organization enables students to gain essential work skills and provides employers with the know-how and resources to "Make Experience Matter."

Matt also partners with his wife Erica to help others improve their physical health and financial well-being with Isagenix nutrition and wellness solutions.

He began his career in marketing communications working for some of Philadelphia's most prominent agencies where he assisted nearly 100 companies, including through his own firm, Z Communication, Inc., which he started in 2002.

He is a frequent lecturer at colleges, universities, professional associations and civic organizations and a published author on a number of related topics.

Matt earned his B.A. in Journalism from Temple University in 1989. He and Erica reside in Bucks County, Pennsylvania with their savvy teenagers, Jake and Greta.

Made in the USA
Middletown, DE
26 June 2021